Editors
Eric Migliaccio
Heather Douglas

Contributing Editor—Canada
Jennifer Dorval

Managing Editor
Ina Massler Levin, M.A.

Illustrators
Renée Christine Yates
Sue Fullam

Cover Artist
Brenda DiAntonis

Art Production Manager
Kevin Barnes

Imaging
Craig Gunnell
Nathan P. Rivera

Publisher
Mary D. Smith, M.S. Ed.

Author

Jodene Lynn Smith, M.A.

Teacher Created Resources, Inc.
6421 Industry Way
Westminster, CA 92683
www.teachercreated.com
ISBN 13: 978-1-4206-2740-1
©2007 Teacher Created Resources, Inc.
Made in U.S.A.

Table of Contents

Introduction

To Teachers and Parents,

The wealth of knowledge a person gains throughout his or her lifetime is impossible to measure, and it will certainly vary from person to person. However, regardless of the scope of knowledge, the foundation for all learning remains a constant. All that we know and think throughout our lifetimes is based upon fundamentals, and these fundamentals are the basic skills upon which all learning develops. *Mastering Kindergarten Skills* is a book that reinforces a variety of kindergarten skills:

✳ **Language Arts**   ✳ **Math**   ✳ **Basic Skills**

This book was written with the wide range of skills and ability levels of kindergarten students in mind. Both teachers and parents can benefit from the variety of pages provided in this book. A parent can use the book to work with his or her child to provide an introduction to new material or to reinforce material already familiar to the child. Similarly, a teacher can select pages that provide additional practice for concepts taught in the classroom. When tied to what is being covered in class, pages from this book make great homework reinforcement. The worksheets provided in this book are ideal for use at home, as well as in the classroom. Research shows us that skill mastery comes with exposure and drill. To be internalized, concepts must be reviewed until they become second nature. Parents may certainly foster the classroom experience by exposing their children to the necessary skills whenever possible, and teachers will find that these pages perfectly complement their classroom needs. An answer key (beginning on page 172) provides teachers, parents, and children with a quick method of checking responses to completed worksheets.

Basic skills are utilized every day and in many ways. Make the practice of them part of your children's or students' routines. Such work done now will benefit them throughout their lives.

Caring for Books

Directions: Color the pictures that show how to take good care of books.

Return Books

Looking at Books

Directions: Have an adult help you answer the questions below. Use the book cover shown in the picture or your own book.

1. What is the title?

_____

- -

_____

2. How many words are in the title?

_____

- -

_____

3. Who is the author?

_____

- -

_____

4. Tell an adult what you think this book will be about.

Letter, Word, or Number?

Directions: Circle the letters. Underline the words. Put an **X** on the numbers.

A   dog   C

v   3

                q

yes

                              no
              7

f   4

                        L

        t   8

                                W
                    r

    z

                              2
    5   cat

Check the Sounds

Directions: Say the name for each picture. Put a check in a box for each sound you hear in the word.

Example:

1	2	3	4
✓	✓	✓	

1.

1	2	3	4

6.

1	2	3	4

2.

1	2	3	4

7.

1	2	3	4

3.

1	2	3	4

8.

1	2	3	4

4.

1	2	3	4

9.

1	2	3	4

5.

1	2	3	4

10.

1	2	3	4

Letters Make Words

Directions: Circle the beginning letter of each word below.

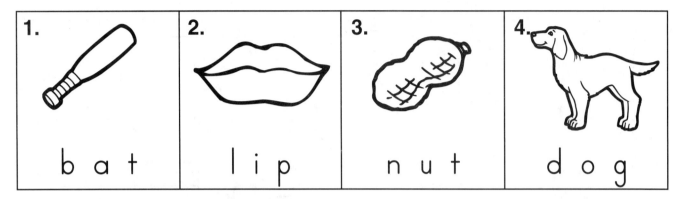

1. b a t
2. l i p
3. n u t
4. d o g

Directions: Circle the middle letter of each word below.

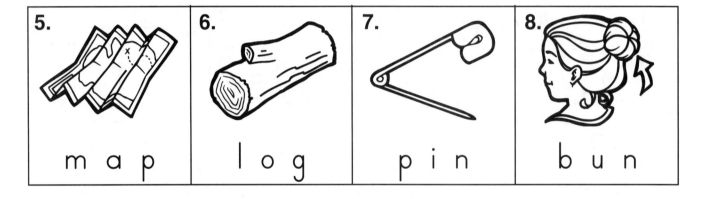

5. m a p
6. l o g
7. p i n
8. b u n

Directions: Circle the ending letter of each word below.

9. t u b
10. m o p
11. w e b
12. f a n

Letter, Word, or Sentence?

Directions: Read each item below. Circle if it is a letter, word, or sentence.

1. dig	letter word sentence	
2. m	letter word sentence	
3. Here is a hen.	letter word sentence	
4. rag	letter word sentence	
5. t	letter word sentence	
6. The kids had fun.	letter word sentence	
7. win	letter word sentence	
8. v	letter word sentence	

Words

Directions: Read the story below. Draw a circle around each word. Write the number of words in each sentence in the box at the end of each line.

The Job

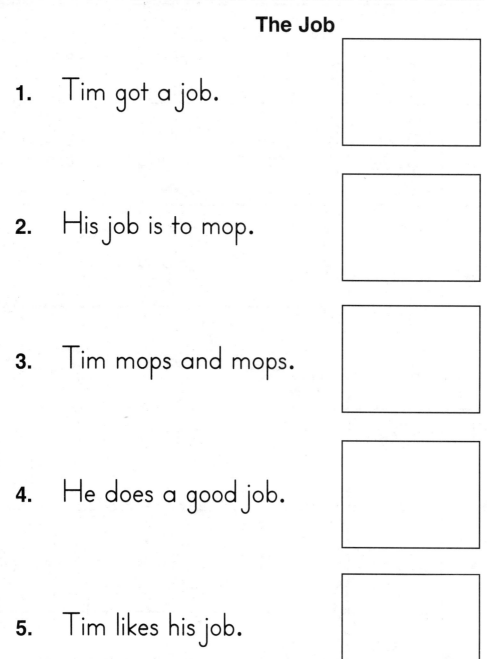

1. Tim got a job.

2. His job is to mop.

3. Tim mops and mops.

4. He does a good job.

5. Tim likes his job.

Note: An adult may read the story out loud if the child cannot read it independently. Have the child point to each word as it is read.

One Sound at a Time

Directions: Use a piece of paper to cover up the pictures. Say the sounds in the words one at a time. Then say the sounds together quickly. Uncover the picture to check the word you read.

1. c-a-n

2. w-i-g

3. d-o-t

4. p-a-n

5. n-e-t

6. h-e-n

7. f-o-x

8. b-a-g

9. n-u-t

10. p-i-n

Syllable Count

Directions: Say the name for each picture. Count how many syllables are in the word. Circle the correct answer.

1. | 2 3

2. 2 3 | 4

3. | 2 3

4. 3 4 5

5. 2 3 4

6. | 2 3

7. | 2 3

8. | 2 3

9. 2 3 4

10. | 2 3

11. 2 3 4

12. 2 3 4

Same Beginning Sound

Directions: Say the name for each picture. Color the smiley face if the words begin with the same sound. Color the sad face if the words do not begin with the same sound.

Phonemic Awareness

Doesn't Belong

Directions: Say the name of the pictures in each row. Color the two pictures that begin with the same sound. Cross off the picture that begins with a different sound.

Same Ending Sound

Directions: Say the name of the picture in the first box. Color the pictures in that row that end with the same sound.

Phonemic Awareness

Beginning or Ending Sound

Directions: Say the name for each picture. Draw a line from the picture to the nail if the word begins with the same sound as the word "nail." Draw a line from the picture to the can if the word ends with the same sound as the word "can."

1.

Begins with N

5.

2.

6.

3.

Ends with N

7.

4.

8.

Same Middle Sound

Directions: Say the name of the picture in the first box. Color the picture in the second box if it has the same middle sound. Put an **X** on the picture if it has a different middle sound.

Rhymes or Not?

Directions: Say the names for each pair of pictures. Color the smiley face if the words rhyme. Color the sad face if the words do not rhyme.

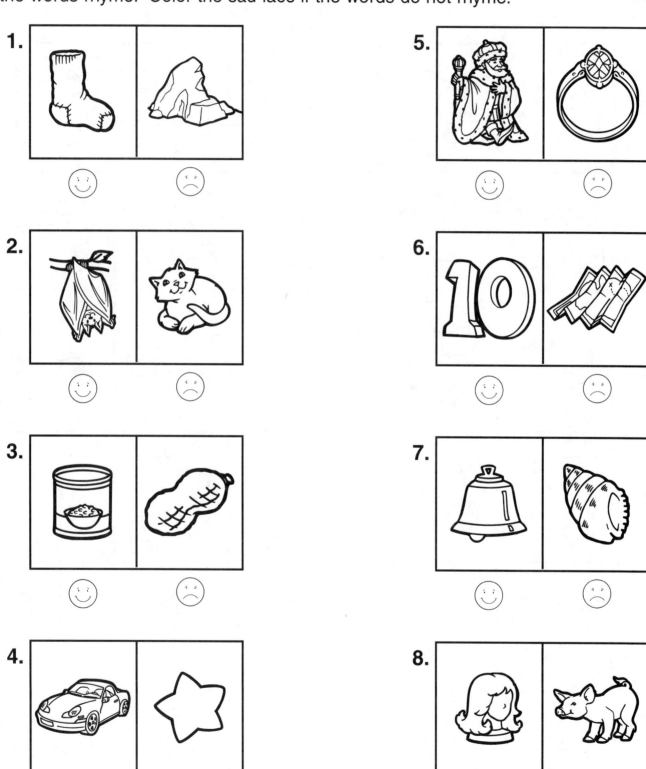

Find Three Rhymes

Directions: Say the name of the picture in the first box. Color the three pictures in each row that rhyme with the name of the picture in the box.

1.

2.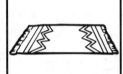

3.

4.

5.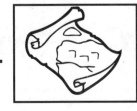

Find the Clown

Directions: Complete the picture by connecting the dots in alphabetical order. Color the clown.

Alpha-Bear

Directions: Complete the picture by connecting the dots in alphabetical order. Color the bear.

Mitten Match

Directions: Match the uppercase and lowercase letters by coloring the mittens the same color. Use a different color for each pair of mittens.

Letter Match

Directions: Draw a line from each uppercase letter to the lowercase letter that matches.

1.	B	b	5.	E	m
2.	F	r	6.	M	e
3.	N	f	7.	C	k
4.	R	n	8.	K	c

Directions: Draw a line from each lowercase letter to the uppercase letter that matches.

9.	d	Y	13.	I	G
10.	y	D	14.	w	W
11.	q	Q	15.	g	T
12.	h	H	16.	t	L

Lowercase Letter Match

Directions: Write the matching lowercase letter next to each uppercase letter.

A _ _ _ _ B _ _ _ _ C _ _ _ _ D _ _ _ _

E _ _ _ _ F _ _ _ _ G _ _ _ _ H _ _ _ _

I _ _ _ _ J _ _ _ _ K _ _ _ _ L _ _ _ _

M _ _ _ _ N _ _ _ _ O _ _ _ _ P _ _ _ _

Q _ _ _ _ R _ _ _ _ S _ _ _ _ T _ _ _ _

U _ _ _ _ V _ _ _ _ W _ _ _ _ X _ _ _ _

Y _ _ _ _ Z _ _ _ _

Uppercase Letter Match

Directions: Write the matching uppercase letter next to each lowercase letter.

a _ _ _ _ _   b _ _ _ _ _   c _ _ _ _ _   d _ _ _ _ _

e _ _ _ _ _   f _ _ _ _ _   g _ _ _ _ _   h _ _ _ _ _

i _ _ _ _ _   j _ _ _ _ _   k _ _ _ _ _   l _ _ _ _ _

m _ _ _ _ _   n _ _ _ _ _   o _ _ _ _ _   p _ _ _ _ _

q _ _ _ _ _   r _ _ _ _ _   s _ _ _ _ _   t _ _ _ _ _

u _ _ _ _ _   v _ _ _ _ _   w _ _ _ _ _   x _ _ _ _ _

y _ _ _ _ _   z _ _ _ _ _

The Letter A

Directions: Color the pictures in the apple that begin with the letter **A**.

Directions: Practice printing the letters and the word.

The Letter B

Directions: Color all of the balloons with a **B** on them with a blue crayon. Color all of the balloons with a **b** on them with a brown crayon.

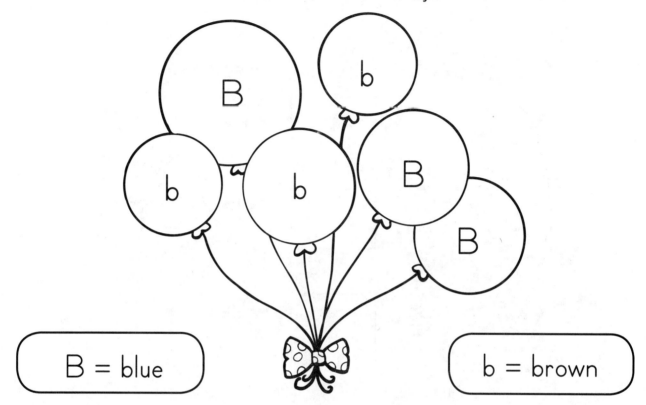

B = blue

b = brown

Directions: Practice printing the letters and the word.

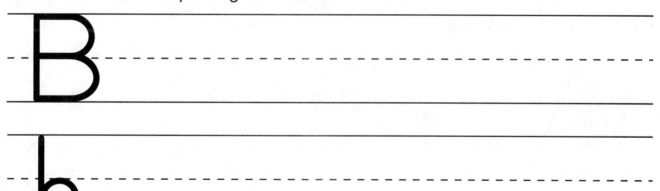

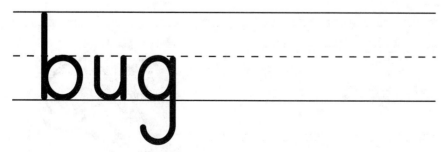

27

The Letter C

Directions: Write the beginning letter for each word. Color the pictures.

1. ☐up

2. ☐arrot

3. ☐at

Directions: Practice printing the letters and the word.

C

c

cat

The Letter D

Directions: Color the pictures in the drum that begin with the letter **D**.

Directions: Practice printing the letters and the word.

The Letter E

Directions: Color the pictures in the egg that begin with the letter **E**.

Directions: Practice printing the letters and the word.

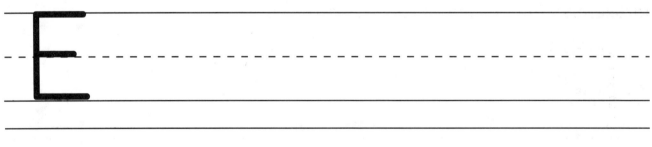

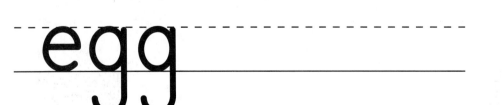

The Letter F

Directions: Color the pictures in the fan that begin with the letter **F**.

Directions: Practice printing the letters and the word.

The Letter G

Directions: Write the beginning letter for each word. Color the pictures.

1.  [ ] um

2.  [ ] oat

3.  [ ] as

Directions: Practice printing the letters and the word.

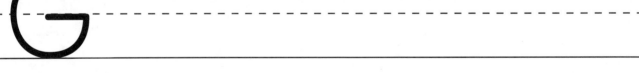

G

g

gum

The Letter H

Directions: Color the pictures in the heart that begin with the letter **H**.

Directions: Practice printing the letters and the word.

The Letter I

Directions: Color the pictures in the igloo that begin with the letter **I**.

Directions: Practice printing the letters and the word.

I

i

in

34   ©*Teacher Created Resources, Inc.*

The Letter J

Directions: Color the pictures in the jellybean that begin with the letter **J**.

Directions: Practice printing the letters and the word.

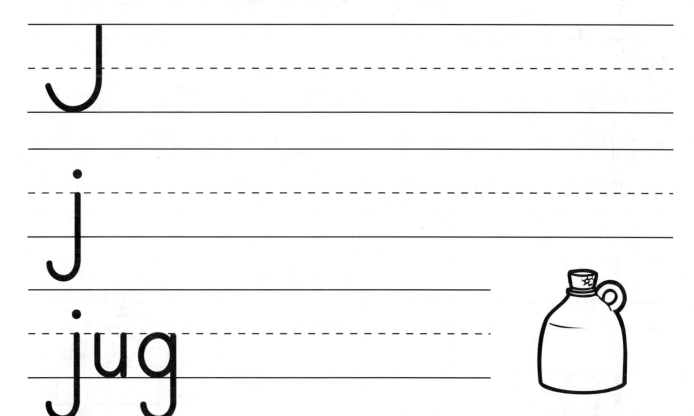

The Letter K

Directions: Write the beginning letter for each word. Color the pictures.

1.  ☐ ing

2.  ☐ ite

3.  ☐ iss

Directions: Practice printing the letters and the word.

The Letter L

Directions: Color each box that has an uppercase **L** with a red crayon. Color each box that has a lowercase **l** with a blue crayon.

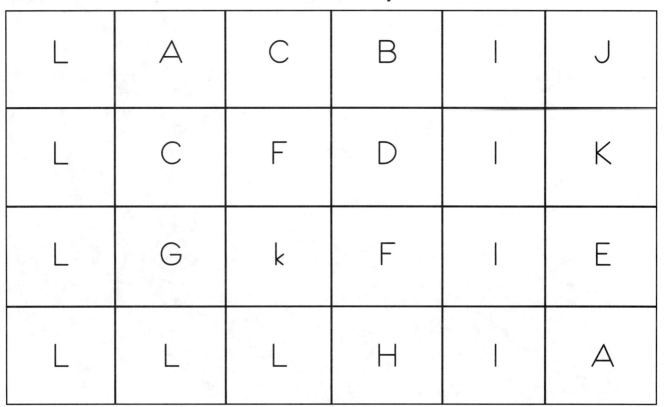

L	A	C	B	l	J
L	C	F	D	l	K
L	G	k	F	l	E
L	L	L	H	l	A

Directions: Practice printing the letters and the word.

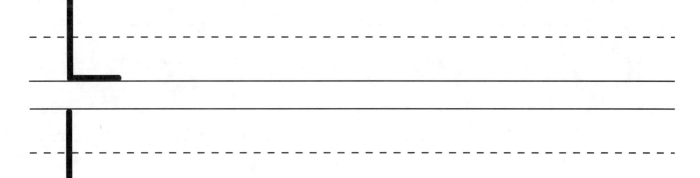

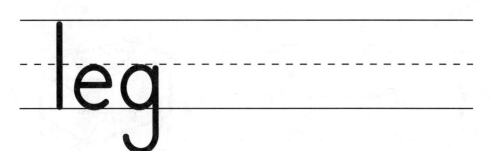

leg

The Letter M

Directions: Color the pictures in the moon that begin with the letter **M**.

Directions: Practice printing the letters and the word.

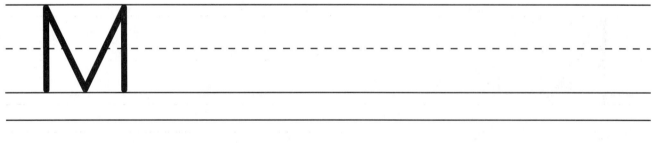

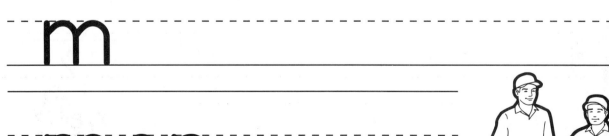

The Letter N

Directions: Color the nuts with the uppercase **N** or lowercase **n** inside. Color the squirrel.

Directions: Practice printing the letters and the word.

The Letter O

Directions: Color the pictures in the olive that begin with the letter **O**.

Directions: Practice printing the letters and the word.

The Letter P

Directions: Color the pictures in the pot that begin with the letter **P**.

Directions: Practice printing the letters and the word.

P

p

pig

The Letter Q

Directions: Color each box that has an uppercase letter **Q** with a green crayon. Color each box that has a lowercase letter **q** with a yellow crayon.

Q	q	G	Q	q	g
q	G	Q	q	g	Q
Q	q	G	Q	q	G
q	G	Q	q	g	Q

Q = green   q = yellow

Directions: Practice printing the letters and the word.

Q

q

queen

The Letter R

Directions: Write the beginning letter for each word. Color the pictures.

1. 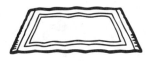 ☐ ug

2.  ☐ ing

3.  ☐ ip

Directions: Practice printing the letters and the word.

R

r

rat

The Letter S

Directions: Color each box that has an uppercase or lowercase **S** with a blue crayon.

P	S	s	S	V	D	d	G	I
H	S	R	M	L	F	K	e	J
k	s	S	S	p	s	S	s	p
r	B	T	s	K	S	s	S	P
N	S	s	S	C	S	s	s	f

Directions: Practice printing the letters and the word.

S

s

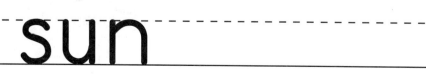

The Letter T

Directions: Color the pictures in the turtle that begin with the letter **T**.

Directions: Practice printing the letters and the word.

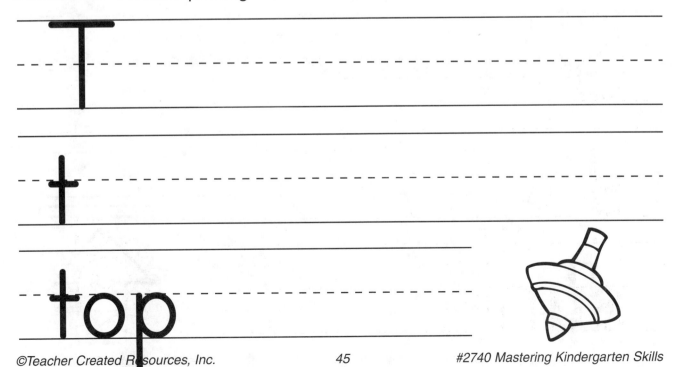

The Letter U

Directions: Color the pictures in the umbrella that begin with the letter **U**.

Directions: Practice printing the letters and the word.

The Letter V

Directions: Color the pictures in the van that begin with the letter **V**.

Directions: Practice printing the letters and the word.

The Letter W

Directions: Write the beginning letter for each word. Color the pictures.

1.  ☐ eb

2.  ☐ ing

3.  ☐ ag

Directions: Practice printing the letters and the word.

W

w

wig

48

The Letter X

Directions: Say the name for the pictures in the boxes. Color the pictures that have the **/x/** sound.

Directions: Practice printing the letters and the word.

X

x

six

The Letter Y

Directions: Write the beginning letter for each word. Color the pictures.

1.  ☐ ell

2.  ☐ arn

3.  ☐ ellow

Directions: Practice printing the letters and the word.

Y

y

yo-yo

The Letter Z

Directions: Color each box that has an uppercase or lowercase **Z** with a blue crayon.

Z	z	Z	Z	Z	m	D	n	o
R	o	R	z	T	Y	g	P	r
S	N	Z	t	O	P	z	Z	Z
T	z	O	n	y	k	A	Z	y
z	Z	z	Z	z	L	z	Z	z

Directions: Practice printing the letters and the word.

Z

z

ZOO

Beginning Sound Match

Directions: Color the pictures in each row that begin with the letter shown.

1. B

2. F

3. L

4. M

5. R

6. S

52

Which Beginning Sound?

Directions: Say the name for each picture. Circle the letter that makes the beginning sound for each word.

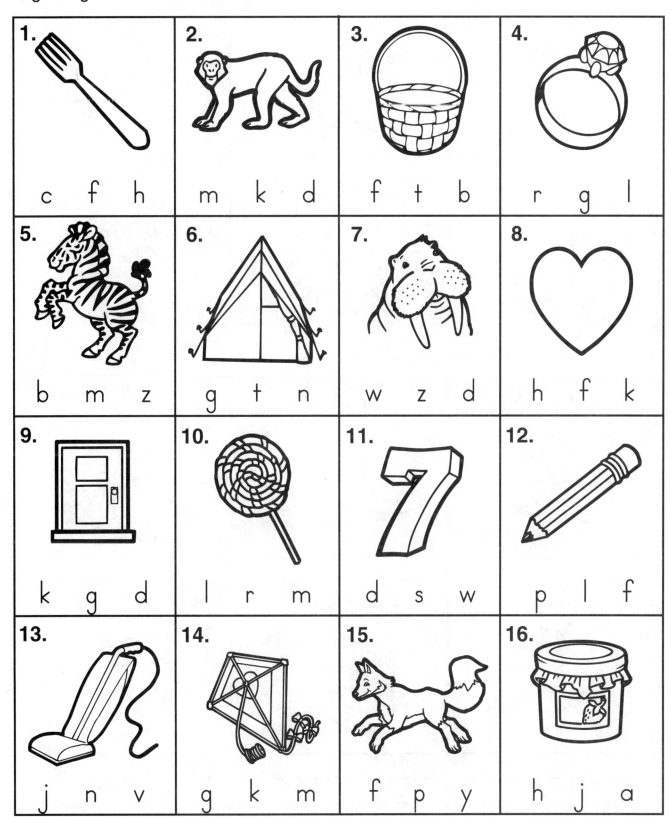

1. c f h
2. m k d
3. f t b
4. r g l
5. b m z
6. g t n
7. w z d
8. h f k
9. k g d
10. l r m
11. d s w
12. p l f
13. j n v
14. g k m
15. f p y
16. h j a

Write the Beginning Sound

Directions: Say the name for each picture. Write the missing letter that represents its beginning sound. Trace the whole word.

1. _ebra	2. _oose	3. _izard
4. _angaroo	5. _urtle	6. _orse
7. _iger	8. _eaver	9. _orcupine
10. _alrus	11. _nake	12. _abbit

Write New Words

Directions: Add the beginning sound shown in the first box of each row in order to make a new word. Practice reading the new words.

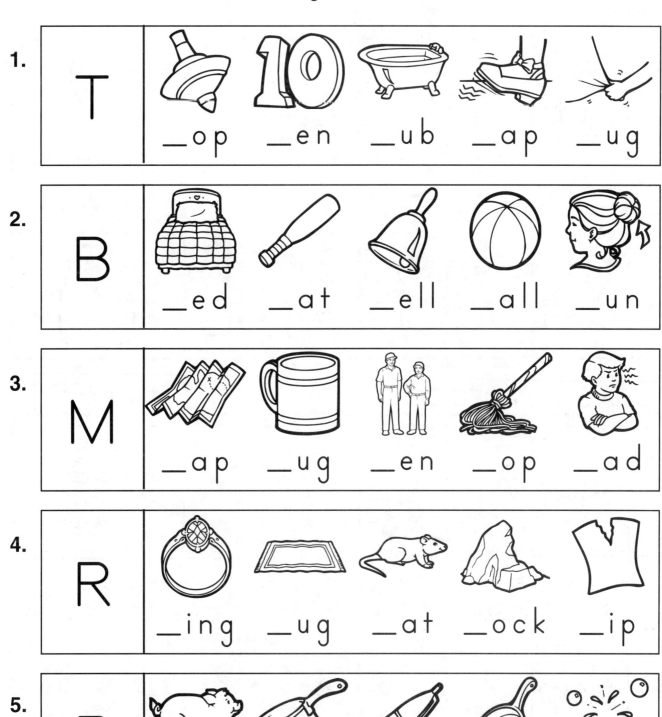

1. T   _op   _en   _ub   _ap   _ug

2. B   _ed   _at   _ell   _all   _un

3. M   _ap   _ug   _en   _op   _ad

4. R   _ing   _ug   _at   _ock   _ip

5. P   _ig   _ot   _en   _an   _op

Change One Sound

Directions: Say the name for each picture. Write the sounds you hear. Use the word family at the beginning of each row to help you spell. Read the rhyming words.

1.

2.

3.

4.
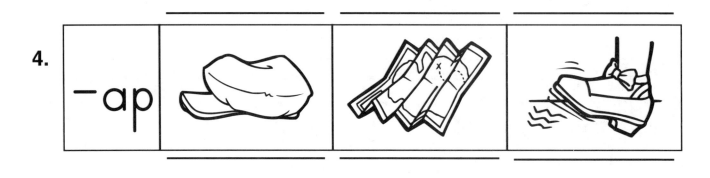

56

Sound It Out

Directions: Say the name for each picture. Write the letter for the beginning sound. Read the new word.

1.  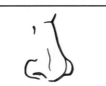   

___ ___ ___

2.     

___ ___ ___

3.   

___ ___ ___

4. 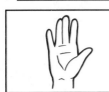    

___ ___ ___

5.      

___ ___ ___

6.   

___ ___ ___

Change the Beginning Sound

Directions: Make a new word. Change the letter that makes the beginning sound. Write the new words on the lines.

1.

Change | met | to | [jet image] | _____

2.

Change | fog | to | [dog image] | _____

3.

Change | pat | to | [hat image] | _____

4.

Change | run | to | [sun image] | _____

5.

Change | win | to | [pin image] | _____

6.

Change | men | to | [ten image] | _____

7.

Change | got | to | [dot image] | _____

8.

Change | tap | to | [map image] | _____

58

Ending Sound

Directions: Say the name for each picture. Write the letter for its ending sound.

1.	2.	3.	4.
5.	6.	7.	8.
9.	10.	11.	12.
13.	14.	15.	16.

What Am I?

Directions: Circle the word that names the picture in each box.

1. fan fat	**2.** map man	**3.** cut cub
4. pen pet	**5.** lot log	**6.** pit pin
7. sub sun	**8.** web wet	**9.** dog dot

60

Change the Ending

Directions: Say the name for each picture. Write the letter for it's ending sound.
Read each pair of words.t.

1.  ma____

    ma____

4.  we____

    we____

2.  do____

    do____

5.  ha____

    ha____

3.  hu____

    hu____

6.  ca____

    ca____

Change the Ending Sound

Directions: Make a new word. Change the letter that makes the ending sound. Write the new word on the line.

1.

Change | bet | to

2.

Change | dot | to

3.

Change | hug | to

4.

Change | fit | to

5.

Change | pet | to

6.

Change | man | to

7.

Change | cop | to

8.

Change | rub | to

Beginning and Ending Sounds

Directions: Say the name for each picture. Write the letter for its beginning sound and its ending sound.

1. _____ i _____
2. _____ o _____
3. _____ a _____
4. _____ e _____

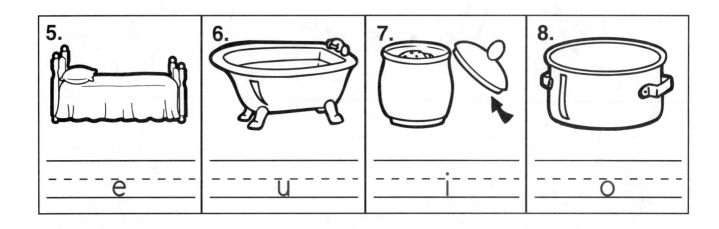

5. _____ e _____
6. _____ u _____
7. _____ i _____
8. _____ o _____

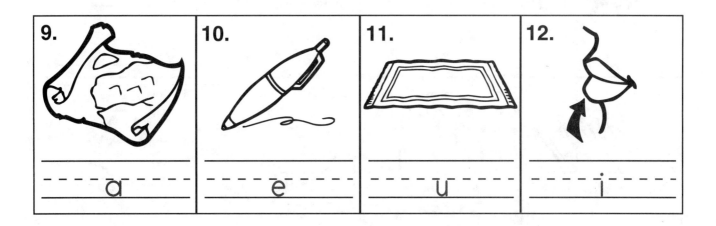

9. _____ a _____
10. _____ e _____
11. _____ u _____
12. _____ i _____

Which Position?

Directions: Say the name of each picture. Circle the first, middle, or last letter to show where you hear it in the word.

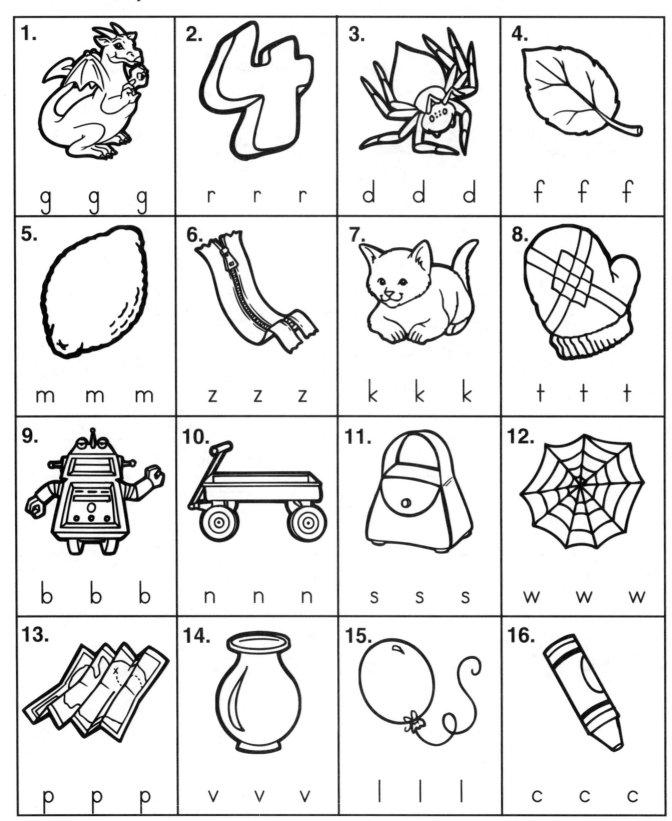

Vowels

Short "A" Words

Directions: Say the name of each picture. Write the beginning, middle, and ending sound for each word. Look at the middle sound of each word when you are done.

1.

2.

3.

4.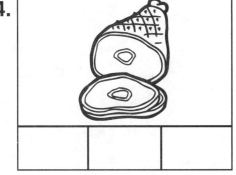

5.

6.

7.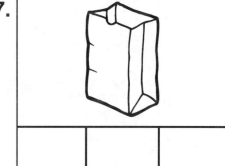

8.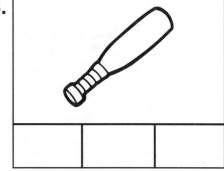

Short "A" Sentences

Directions: Read each sentence. Draw a line from each sentence to the picture that shows that sentence.

1.

A cat has a map.

2.

A dad has a van.

3.

A man has a hat.

4.

A rat has a can.

Short "E" Words

Directions: Say the name of each picture. On the line, write the word that names the picture. Use the words from the box below to help you.

ten	net	bed	hen
nest	men	bell	jet

1. _____

2. _____

3. _____

4. _____

5. _____

6. _____

7. _____

8. _____

Short "E" Sentences

Directions: Read each sentence. Draw a line from each sentence to the picture that shows that sentence.

1.

   The hen has a bell.

2.

   Ned is wet.

3.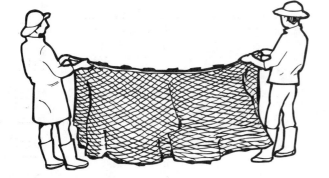

   The nest has eggs.

4.

   The men have a net.

Short "I" Words

Directions: Look at each picture. Read the sentence. Write the word that completes the sentences so that it matches the picture.

1.		It is a _____.		pin / pat / pan
2.		It is a _____.		wit / wag / wig
3.		It is a _____.		ring / rag / rung
4.		It is a _____.		hit / hill / hall
5.		It is a _____.		pup / pop / pig
6.		It is a _____.		lid / lip / lad

Short "I" Sentences

Directions: Read each sentence. Draw a line from each sentence to the picture that shows that sentence.

1.

The kid can dig.

2.

The king can sit.

3.

The kid has a bib.

4.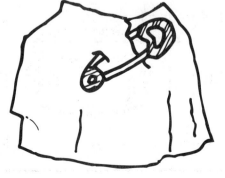

The pin will fix the rip.

Short "O" Words

Directions: Say the name of each picture. Circle the word that names the picture.

1.	2.	3.
dot dog dat	pup pop pot	lot leg log

4.	5.	6.
hat hip hop	dot dog dig	sop sick sock

7.	8.	9.
cot cat cop	tot tap top	lock lack lot

10.	11.	12.
hug hog hot	rack rug rock	pot pop pat

Short "O" Sentences

Directions: Read each sentence. Draw a line from each sentence to the picture that shows that sentence.

1.

The dog is on a log.

2.

The dog is on top.

3.

The dog can mop.

4.

The dog can jog.

Short "U" Words

Directions: Say the name for each picture. Write the beginning, middle, and ending sound. Practice reading each word.

1.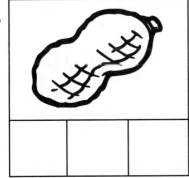

2.

3.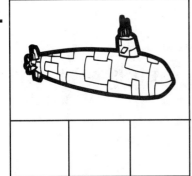

4.

5.

6.

7.

8.

Short "U" Sentences

Directions: Read each sentence. Draw a line from each sentence to the picture that shows that sentence.

1.

The cub can run.

2.

The tub is on the rug.

3.

The mug is by the bun.

4.

The bug is in the sun.

Vowels

What Is the Vowel?

Directions: Say the name of each picture. Color the box with the letter that matches the short vowel sound.

Missing Vowel

Directions: Say the name of each picture. Write the missing vowel.

1.

h __ m

2.

n __ st

3.

h __ t

4.

b __ s

5.

l __ ck

6.

l __ p

7.

b __ d

8.

n __ t

9.

h __ p

Short Vowel Sort

Directions: Read the words in the list. Write each word in the shape that matches the short vowel sound in the word.

tin	sat	pit
dad	run	tan
hum	did	lot
hop	den	yet
fed	fog	dug

Short "u"

Short "a"

Short "e"

Short "o"

Short "i"

Long "A"

Directions: Use the words in the box below to complete the sentences. Write the rhyming words.

gate	rain	rake	tail
cake	mail	skate	train

1.

_ _ _ _ _ _ _ _ _   rhymes with   _ _ _ _ _ _ _

2.

_ _ _ _ _ _ _ _ _   rhymes with   _ _ _ _ _ _ _

3.

_ _ _ _ _ _ _ _ _   rhymes with   _ _ _ _ _ _ _

4.

_ _ _ _ _ _ _ _ _   rhymes with   _ _ _ _ _ _ _

78

Long "E"

Directions: Say the name for each picture. Write the long "E" word that names the picture. Use the words from the word box to help you.

leaf	key	bee	meat
tea	eel	seal	feet

1.

_____

- - - - - - - - -

_____

2.

_____

- - - - - - - - -

_____

3.

_____

- - - - - - - - -

_____

4.

_____

- - - - - - - - -

_____

5.

_____

- - - - - - - - -

_____

6.

_____

- - - - - - - - -

_____

7.

_____

- - - - - - - - -

_____

8.

_____

- - - - - - - - -

_____

Long "I"

Directions: Say the name of each picture. If you hear the long "I" sound, color the box labeled "long." If you hear the short "I" sound, color the box labeled "short."

1.

| short | long |

2.

| short | long |

3.

| short | long |

4.

| short | long |

5.

| short | long |

6.

| short | long |

7.

| short | long |

8.

| short | long |

9.

| short | long |

Long "O"

Directions: Say the name for each picture. If you hear the long "O" sound, color the box. If you do not hear the long "O" sound, draw an **X** on the picture. Follow the path to help the dog find its bone.

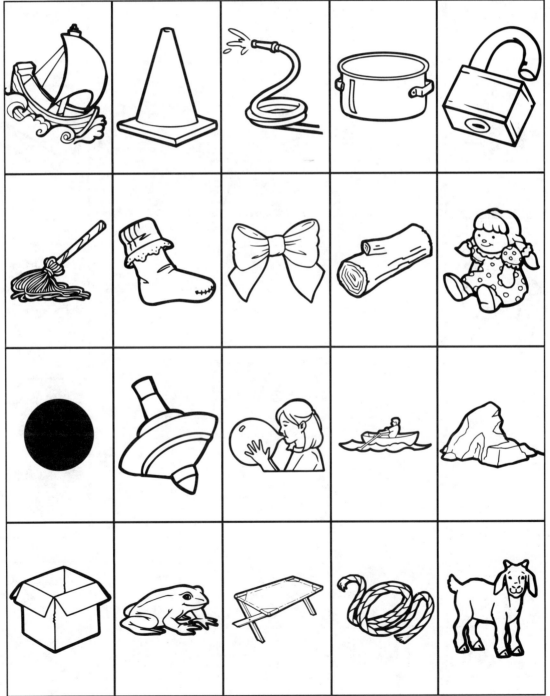

Long "U"

Directions: Say the name for each picture. Draw a line from the picture to the "Short Vowel" box if the word has the short "U" sound. Draw a line from the picture to the "Long Vowel" box if the word has a long "U" sound.

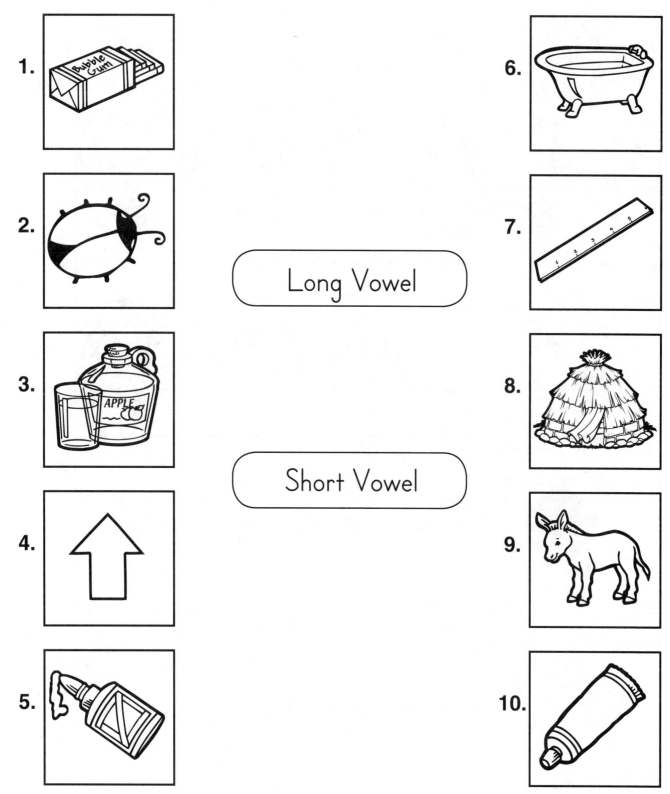

1.

2.

3.

4.

5.

Long Vowel

Short Vowel

6.

7.

8.

9.

10.

82

Long Vowel Review

Directions: Say the name of each picture. Circle the letter that makes the long vowel sound in each word.

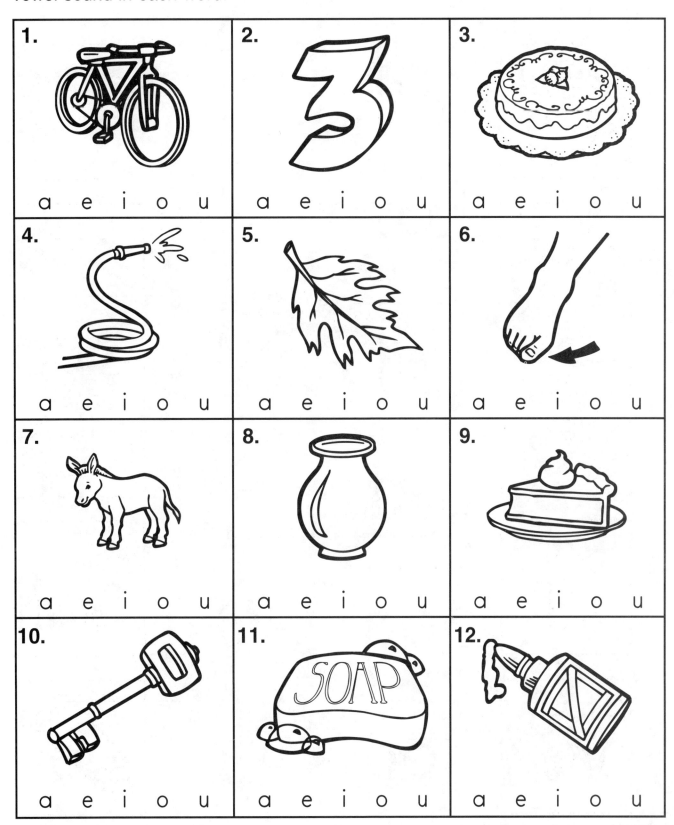

1. a e i o u
2. a e i o u
3. a e i o u
4. a e i o u
5. a e i o u
6. a e i o u
7. a e i o u
8. a e i o u
9. a e i o u
10. a e i o u
11. a e i o u
12. a e i o u

Change a Letter

Directions: Say the name for each picture. Write the letter for its beginning sound. Read each pair of words. Do they rhyme?

1. _____ at

_____ at

2. _____ et

_____ et

3. _____ og

_____ og

4. _____ ig

_____ ig

5. _____ un

_____ un

6. _____ ell

_____ ell

Word Family Pairs

Directions: Match the socks. Read the word on each sock. Find another word from the same word family on another sock. Color the two socks the same color. Use a different color for each pair of socks.

Words in a Family

Directions: Make words in a word family by changing the beginning sound. Use the letter that is in the box at the beginning of the row.

1.

p<u>in</u>

w	
t	
f	
b	

3.

j<u>et</u>

w	
g	
l	
m	

2.

t<u>op</u>

m	
h	
p	
c	

4.

m<u>ug</u>

t	
b	
h	
j	

Word Families

Directions: Say the name for each picture. Write the letters for the sounds you hear in the word. Circle the letters that are the same in all the words. Think of your own word from the same word family. Draw a picture and write the word.

1.

__ __ __

__ __ __

__ __ __

__ __ __

2.

__ __ __

__ __ __

__ __ __

__ __ __

3.

__ __ __

__ __ __

__ __ __

__ __ __

4.

__ __ __

__ __ __

__ __ __

__ __ __

Colors

Directions: Complete each sentence with a word that tells more about the color. Draw a picture of what you write.

A _____ is red.

A _____ is blue.

A _____ is yellow.

A _____ is green.

Writing About Seasons

Directions: Complete the sentences to tell about the seasons. Draw a picture to match each season.

1.

In the fall _____
_____

2.

In the winter _____
_____

3.

In the spring _____
_____

4.

In the summer _____
_____

When I Grow Up

Directions: Write about what you will do when you grow up. Draw a picture to match your writing.

Outside

Directions: Write about something you like to do outside. Draw a picture to go with your writing.

Sight Word: Is

Directions: Trace the word "is." Then, write the word "is" on the lines to complete the sentences.

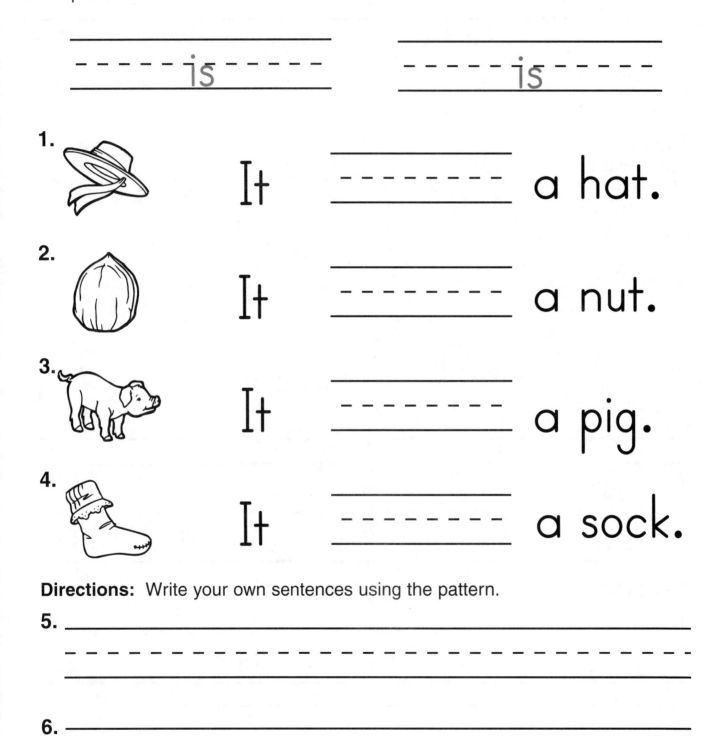

_____ is _____   _____ is _____

1. It _____ a hat.

2. It _____ a nut.

3. It _____ a pig.

4. It _____ a sock.

Directions: Write your own sentences using the pattern.

5. _____

6. _____

Sight Word: See

Directions: Trace the word "see" below. Then write the word "see" on the lines to complete the sentences.

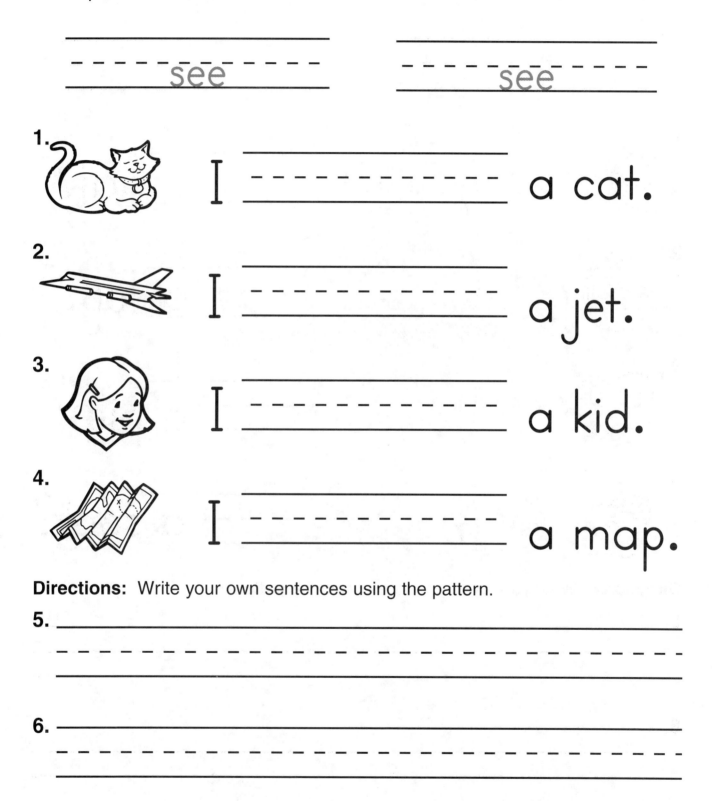

see   see

1. I _____ a cat.

2. I _____ a jet.

3. I _____ a kid.

4. I _____ a map.

Directions: Write your own sentences using the pattern.

5. _____

6. _____

Sight Word: The

Directions: Trace the sight word "the" below. Then write the word "the" on the lines to complete the sentences.

the   the

1. Can you see _____ bug?

2. Can you see _____ log?

3. Can you see _____ sun?

4. Can you see _____ nest?

Directions: Write your own sentences using the pattern.

5. _____

6. _____

Sight Word: This

Directions: Trace the sight word "this" below. Then write the word "this" on the lines to complete the sentences.

This   This

1. _____ is a hen.

2. _____ is a jet.

3. _____ is a pen.

4. _____ is a van.

Directions: Write your own sentences using the pattern.

5. _____

6. _____

Color Words

Directions: Choose the most common color for each picture. Write the name of the color on the line. Use the words in the word box below to help you.

1. _____

5. _____

2. _____

6. _____

3. _____

7. _____

4. _____

8. _____

red	green	brown	purple
orange	blue	black	yellow

Shape Names

Directions: Draw a line from each shape to the word that names that shape.

1.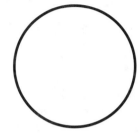

circle

2.

triangle

3.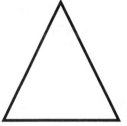

heart

4.

square

5.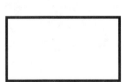

oval

6.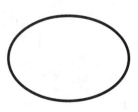

rectangle

Number Names

Directions: Count how many stars are in each box. Write the correct number word on the line. Use the words in the box below to help you.

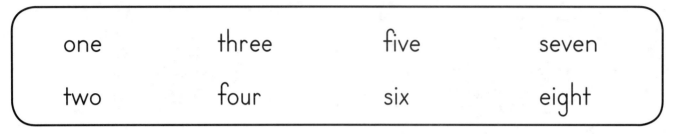

| one | three | five | seven |
| two | four | six | eight |

1. 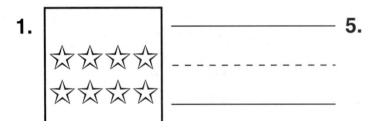 _____   **5.** 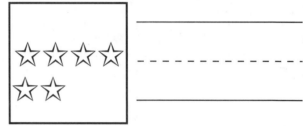 _____

2. _____   **6.** _____

3. _____   **7.** _____

4. _____   **8.** _____

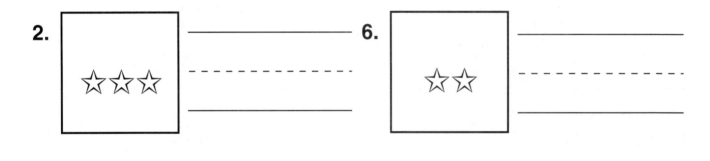
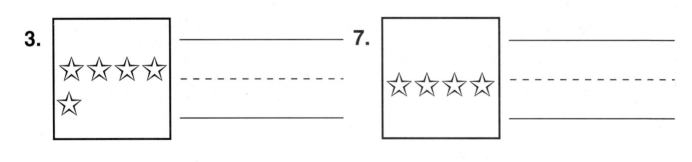
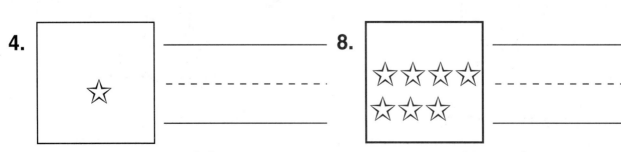

What Color Is It?

Directions: Read the sentences. Color the pictures.

1. The sun is yellow.	**5.** The grass is green.
2. The cat is black.	**6.** The bear is brown.
3. The heart is red.	**7.** The pumpkin is orange.
4. The bird is blue.	**8.** The hat is black.

How Many?

Directions: Read the sentences. Draw a picture to match the sentence.

1. Here are two ♥ s.	**5.** Here are four 🌷 s.
2. Here is one 🎈 .	**6.** Here are six 🖍 s.
3. Here are seven 😀 s.	**7.** Here are three ⭐ s.
4. Here are five 🏀 s.	**8.** Here are ten ● s.

O Animals

Directions: Practice writing the number **0** and the word **zero** on the lines below.

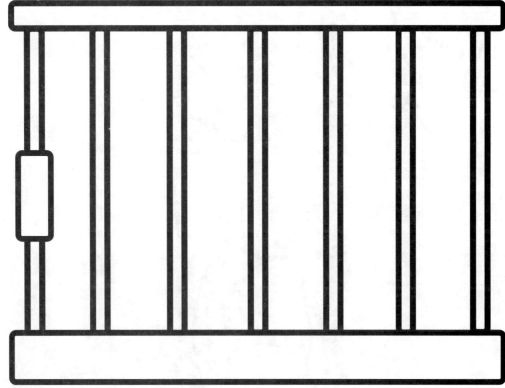

How many animals are in the pen?

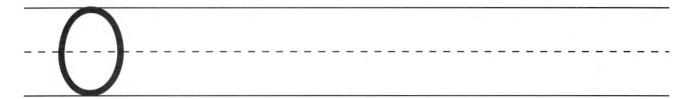

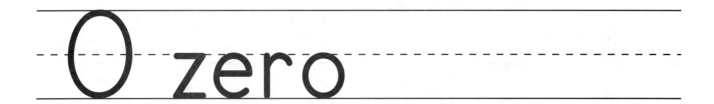

1 Animal

Directions: Practice writing the number **1** and the word **one** on the lines below.

one

one

2 Animals

Directions: Practice writing the number **2** and the word **two** on the lines below.

2

2 two

two

3 Animals

Directions: Practice writing the number **3** and the word **three** on the lines below.

3

3 three

three

4 Animals

Directions: Practice writing the number **4** and the word **four** on the lines below.

4

4 four

four

5 Animals

Directions: Practice writing the number **5** and the word **five** on the lines below.

5

5 five

five

106

6 Animals

Directions: Practice writing the number **6** and the word **six** on the lines below.

6
----

6 six
----

six
----

7 Animals

Directions: Practice writing the number **7** and the word **seven** on the lines below.

7

7 seven

seven

8 Animals

Directions: Practice writing the number **8** and the word **eight** on the lines.

8

8 eight

eight

9 Animals

Directions: Practice writing the number **9** and the word **nine** on the lines below.

q

q nine

nine

10 Animals

Directions: Practice writing the number **10** and the word **ten** on the lines below.

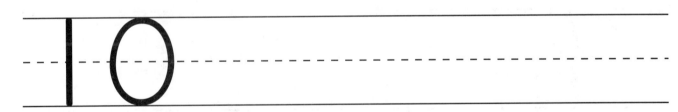

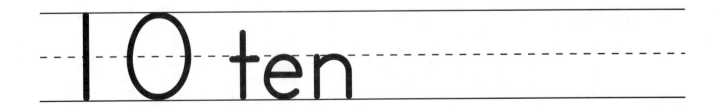

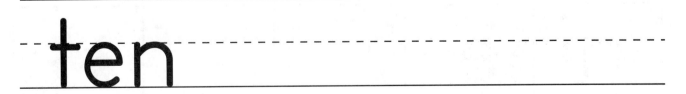

Numbers 1 to 20

Directions: Trace the numbers from 1 to 20 in the first box. Write the numbers from 1 to 20 in the second box.

1	2	3	4	5
6	7	8	9	10
11	12	13	14	15
16	17	18	19	20

1–10 Dot-to-Dot

Directions: Connect the dots to finish the picture. Begin and end at "Start."

1–20 Dot-to-Dot

Directions: Connect the dots to finish the picture. Begin and end at "Start."

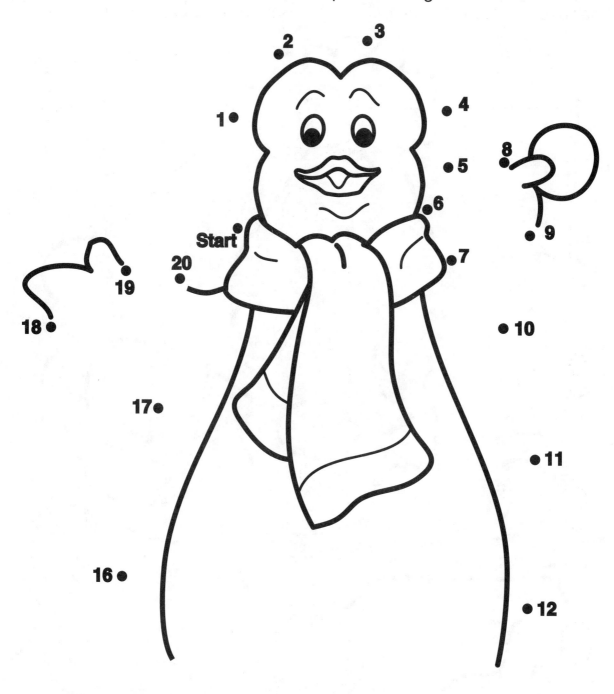

Count the Candles

Directions: Count the number of candles on each birthday cake. Match the number of candles to the number and the word by drawing a line to each.

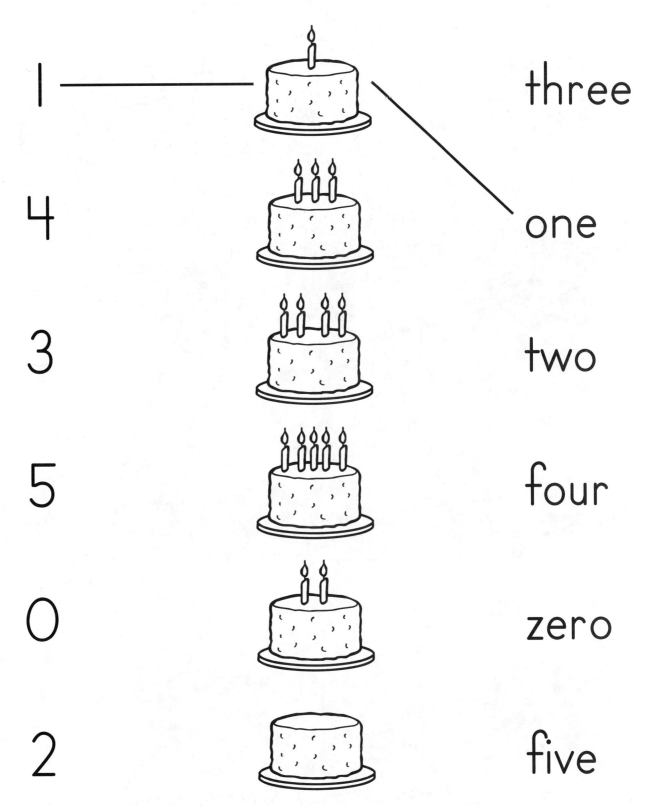

Dots All Around

Directions: Count the number of dots on each ladybug. Write the number in the box.

1.

5.

2.

6.

3.

7.

4.

8.

Fun in the Sun

Directions: Read the number. Trace over the number. Draw the number of objects shown in the box on the right.

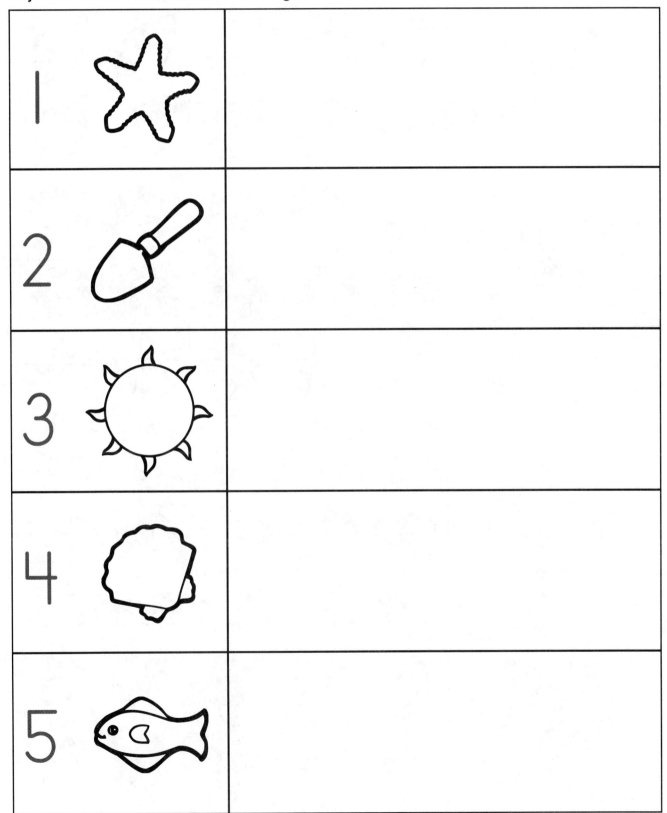

More Fun in the Sun

Directions: Read the number in the first box. Color that many objects in the second box.

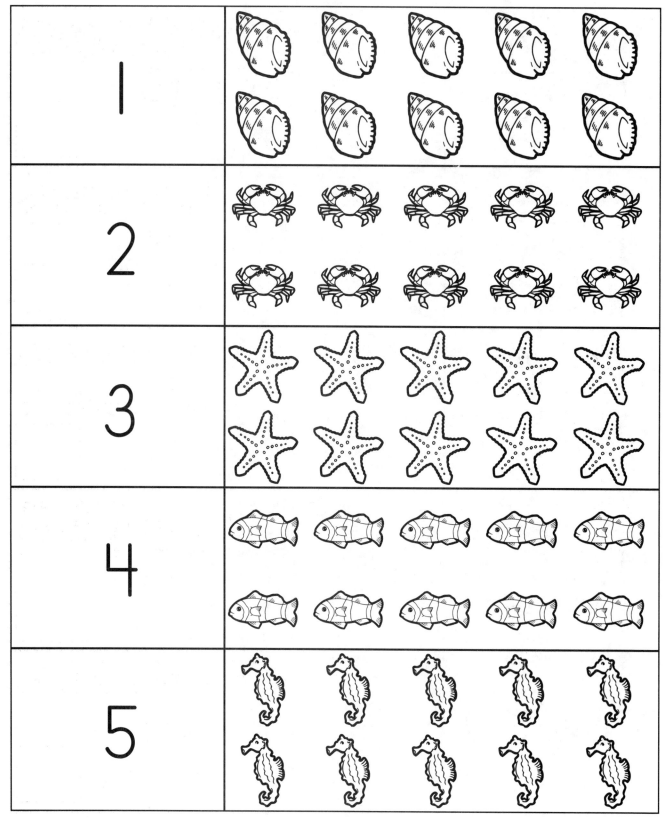

Counting 10–20

Directions: Count how many objects are in each set. Write the number in the box.

1.

6.

2.

7.

3.

8.

4.

9.

5.

10.

More and Less

Directions: Count the objects in each picture. Write the number in the box to the right. Compare the pictures. Color the picture with **more** objects. Draw an **X** on the picture with **less** objects.

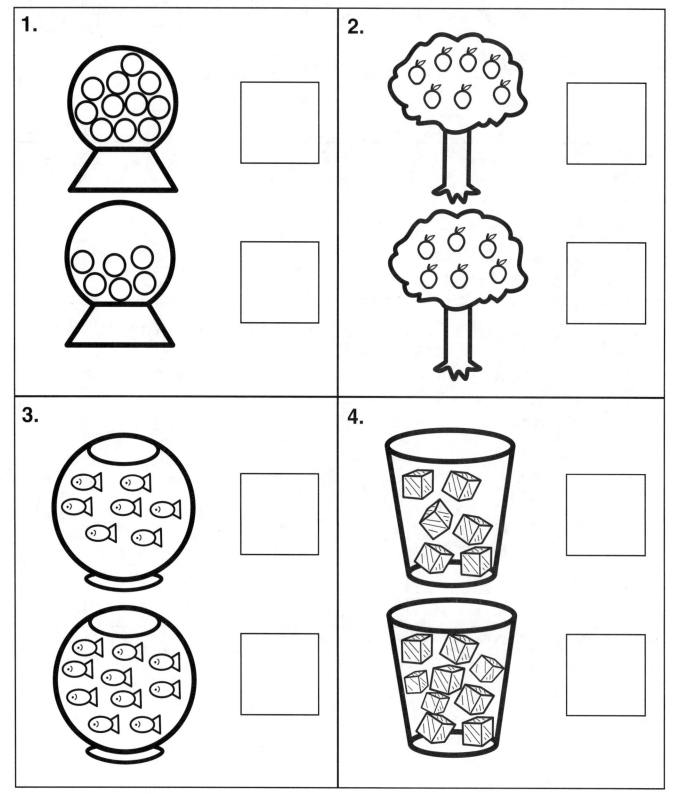

Equal Sets

Directions: Count the objects in each set. Draw an equal set in the box on the right.

1.

2.

3.

4.

5.

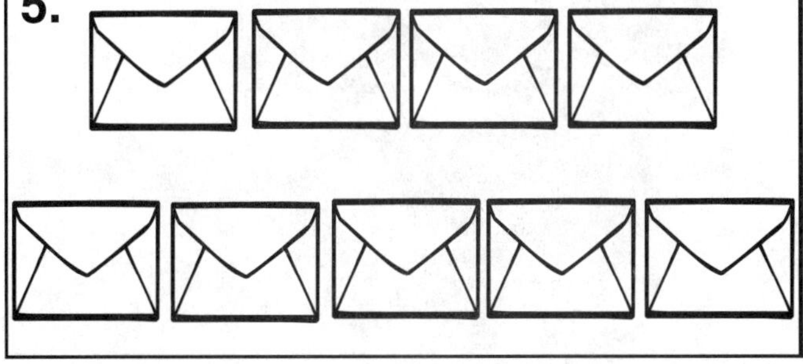

Make Ten

Directions: Count the objects in each set. Draw more, if needed, to make a set of 10.

1.

4.
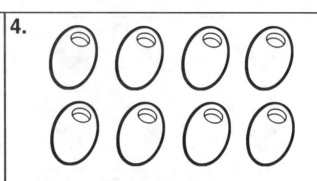

2.

5.
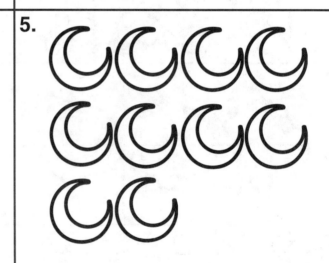

3.

6.

Larger Numbers

Directions: Compare the two numbers in each box. Circle the larger number. Put an **X** on the smaller number.

1. 7 10	**2.** 2 4	**3.** 8 3
4. 12 9	**5.** 18 20	**6.** 14 17
7. 6 13	**8.** 5 1	**9.** 11 4
10. 16 15	**11.** 13 19	**12.** 10 20

Counting by 2s

Directions: Count the mittens. Write the number you say under each mitten.

1.

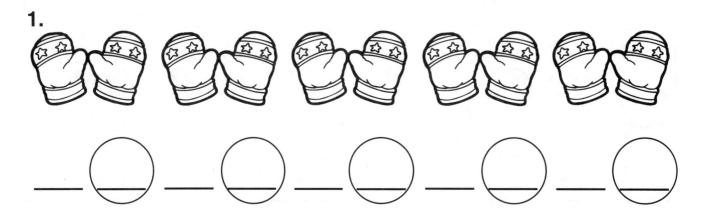

Write the numbers in the circles on the lines below. Practice counting by 2s.

2.

Count the footprints by 2s.

3.

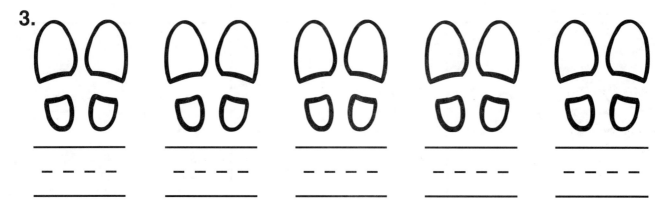

Count the socks by 2s.

4.

Counting by 5s

Directions: Count the fingers. Write the number you say on the line above each finger.

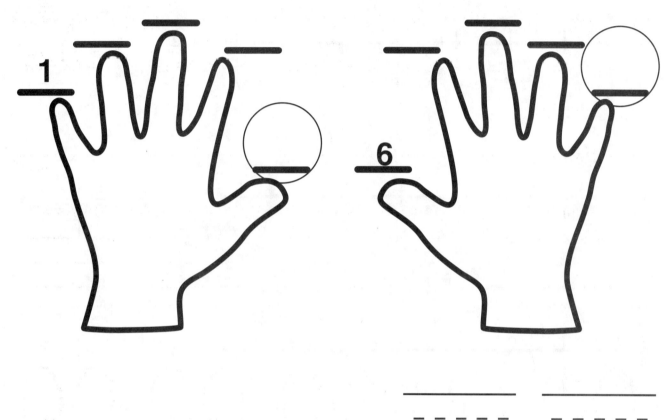

Write the numbers that are in the circles above. _____   _____

Color the boxes of the numbers you say when you count by 5s.

1	2	3	4	5	6	7	8	9	10
11	12	13	14	15	16	17	18	19	20
21	22	23	24	25	26	27	28	29	30

Jump to Add

Directions: Count forward to add. Put your finger where the frog is. Jump forward 1 jump. Write the number you land on.

1.

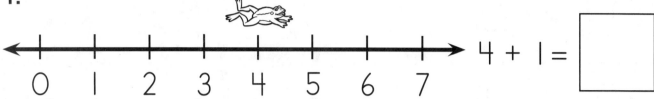

4 + 1 =

2.

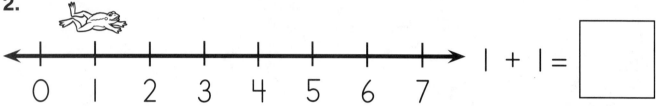

1 + 1 =

3.

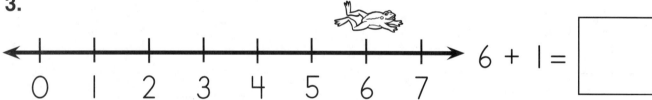

6 + 1 =

4.

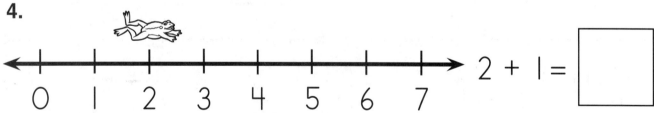

2 + 1 =

5.

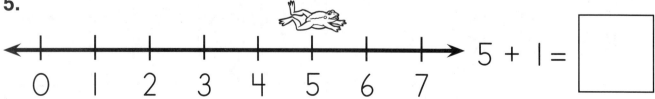

5 + 1 =

Adding Animals

Directions: Look at the pictures. Write how many are in all.

1.

$2 + 1 =$ ▢

5.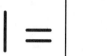

$4 + 1 =$ ▢

2.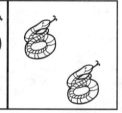

$3 + 2 =$ ▢

6.

$1 + 3 =$ ▢

3.

$2 + 2 =$ ▢

7.

$2 + 4 =$ ▢

4.

$1 + 2 =$ ▢

8.

$2 + 3 =$ ▢

Adding Buttons

Directions: Look at the pictures. Add the buttons together to tell how many there are in all.

1.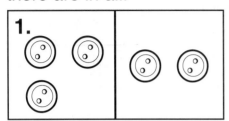

3 + 2 =

2.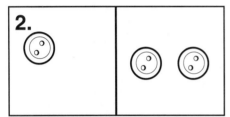

1 + 2 =

3.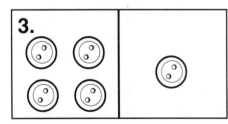

4 + 1 =

4.

2 + 3 =

5.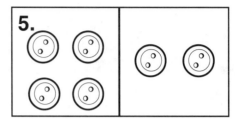

4 + 2 =

6.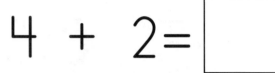

5 + 1 =

7.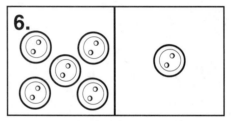

3 + 1 =

8.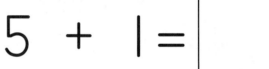

2 + 2 =

Under the Sea

Directions: Look at each picture. Write an addition problem to match the picture.

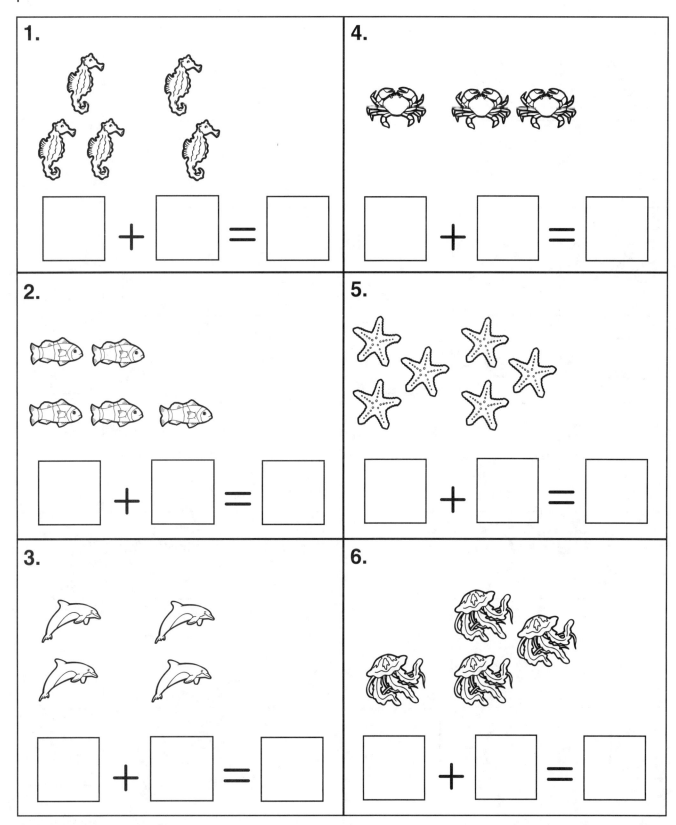

Adding Zero

Directions: Look at each picture. Add 0 animals. Write how many there are in all. What do you notice happens when you add 0?

1.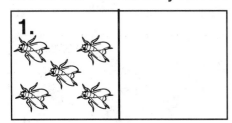

5 + 0=

5.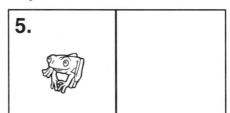

1 + 0=

2.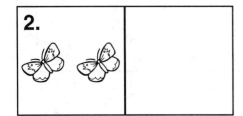

2 + 0=

6.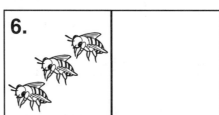

3 + 0=

3.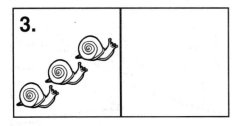

3 + 0=

7.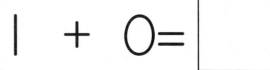

4 + 0=

4.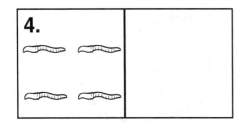

4 + 0=

8.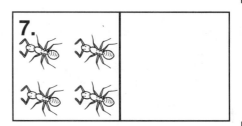

2 + 0=

     130

Pretty Bird

Directions: Add to solve the problems. Use the answer to color the picture using the color code.

4 = red   5 = orange

Busy Bees

Directions: Add to solve the problems below. Count forward on the number line to help.

0 1 2 3 4 5 6 7 8 9 10

1. $4 + 2 = \boxed{}$

2. $7 + 1 = \boxed{}$

3. $5 + 3 = \boxed{}$

4. $8 + 2 = \boxed{}$

5. $3 + 6 = \boxed{}$

6. $2 + 7 = \boxed{}$

7. $9 + 1 = \boxed{}$

8. $4 + 5 = \boxed{}$

9. $2 + 6 = \boxed{}$

10. $8 + 1 = \boxed{}$

Jump Back to Subtract

Directions: Count backward to subtract. Put your finger where the kangaroo is. Jump backward 1 jump. Write the number you land on.

1.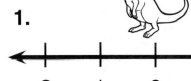

0 1 2 3 4 5 6 7   2 – 1 =

2.

0 1 2 3 4 5 6 7   4 – 1 =

3.

0 1 2 3 4 5 6 7   6 – 1 =

4.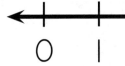

0 1 2 3 4 5 6 7   3 – 1 =

5.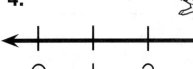

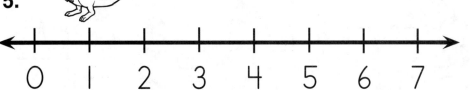

0 1 2 3 4 5 6 7   1 – 1 =

Animal Subtraction

Directions: Look at each picture. Write how many are left.

1.

3 − 1 =

4.

2 − 1 =

2.

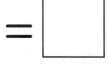

5 − 2 =

5.

3 − 2 =

3.

4 − 3 =

6.

4 − 2 =

134

On the Go

Directions: Look at each picture. Write how many are left.

1.

$$5 - 2 = \boxed{}$$

4.

$$5 - 4 = \boxed{}$$

2.

$$6 - 4 = \boxed{}$$

5.

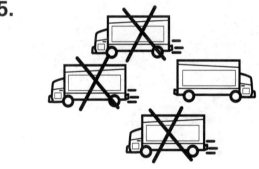

$$4 - 3 = \boxed{}$$

3.

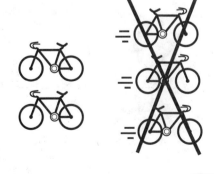

$$5 - 3 = \boxed{}$$

6.

$$6 - 3 = \boxed{}$$

Subtraction Fun

Directions: Look at each picture. Write a subtraction problem to match the picture.

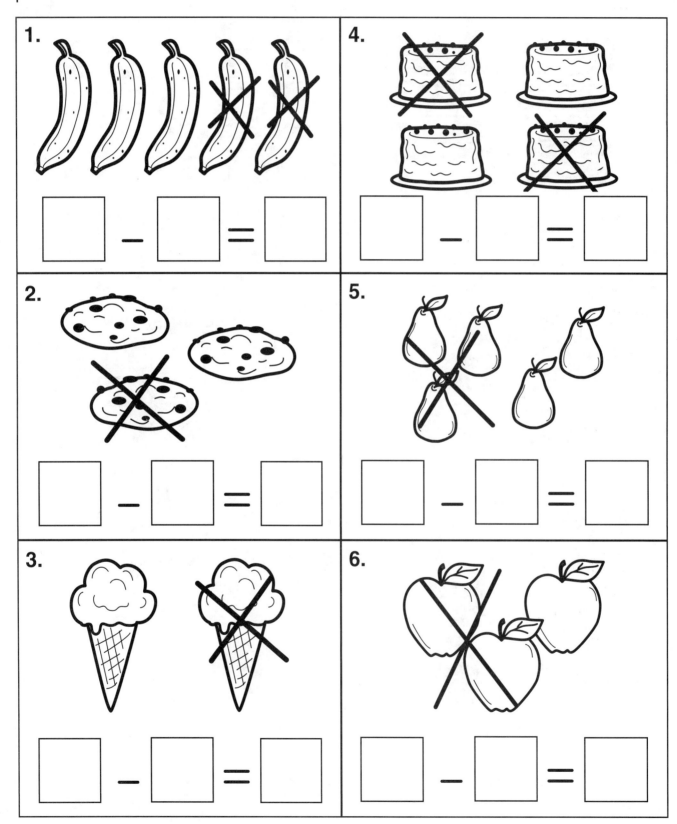

Subtracting Zero

Directions: Look at each picture. Subtract 0 objects. Write how many are left.

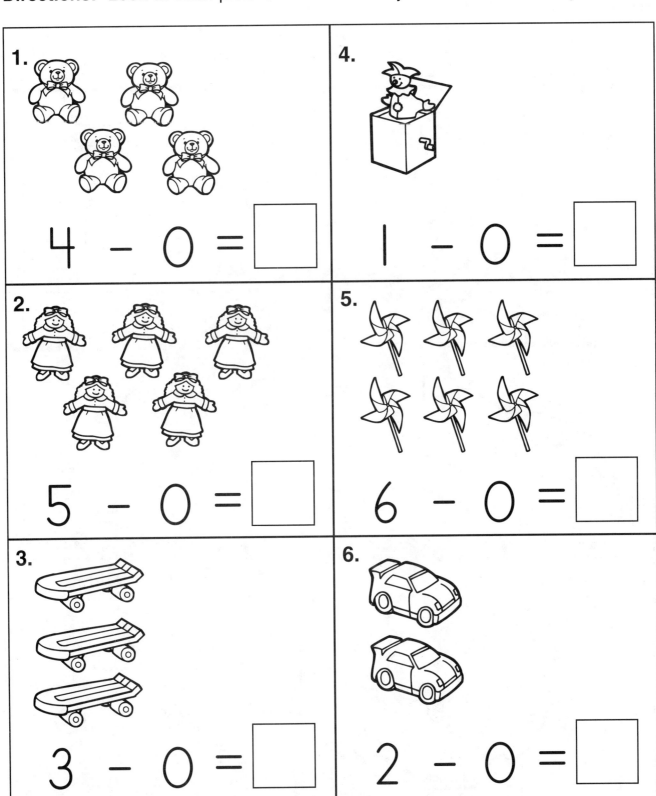

What do you notice when you subtract 0?

Jump for Joy

Directions: Solve the subtraction problems. Use the answer to color the picture using the color code.

1 = red	2 = blue	3 = green	4 = black	5 = brown

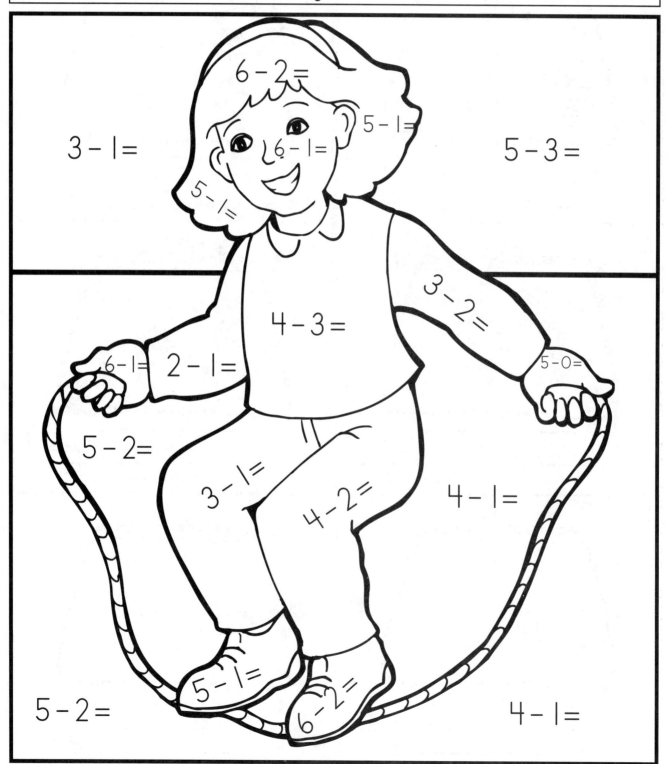

Coin Purses

Directions: Count the coins in the coin purses. Write the amounts on the lines.

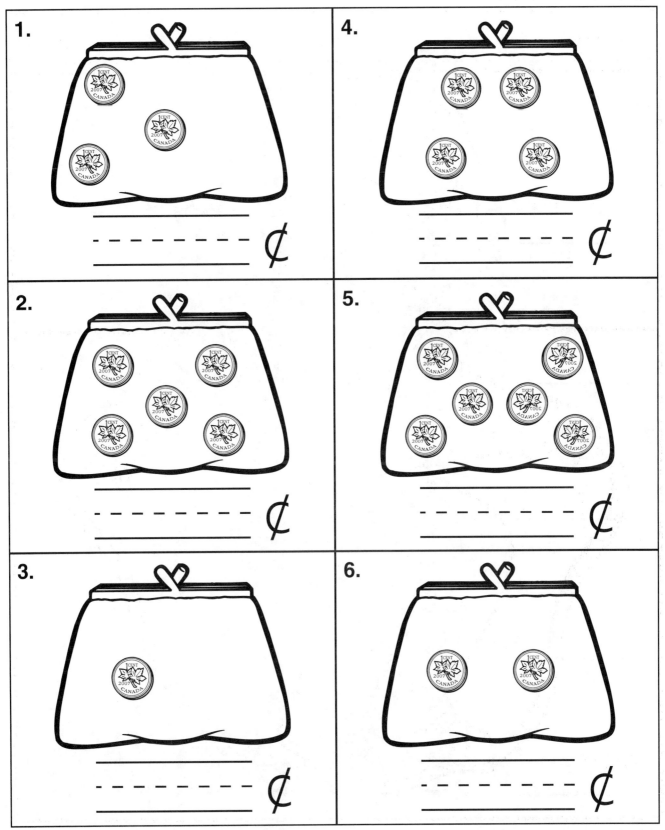

Counting Money

Directions: Count the amount of money in each line. Write the total.

1.

_____ ¢

2.

_____ ¢

3.

_____ ¢

4.

_____ ¢

5.

_____ ¢

6.

_____ ¢

Exchange Toy Show

Directions: Count the coins. Answer the questions.

1.
_____ ¢ 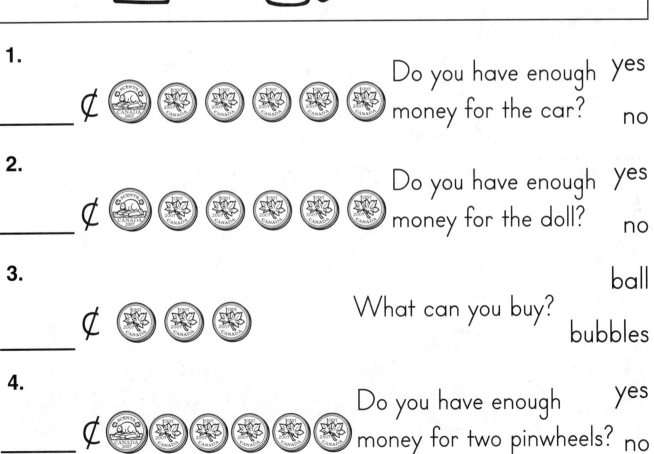 Do you have enough money for the car?   yes   no

2.
_____ ¢ Do you have enough money for the doll?   yes   no

3.
_____ ¢ What can you buy?   ball   bubbles

4.
_____ ¢ Do you have enough money for two pinwheels?   yes   no

Patterns

AB Patterning

Directions: Color each pattern. Complete each pattern by coloring the picture that will come next.

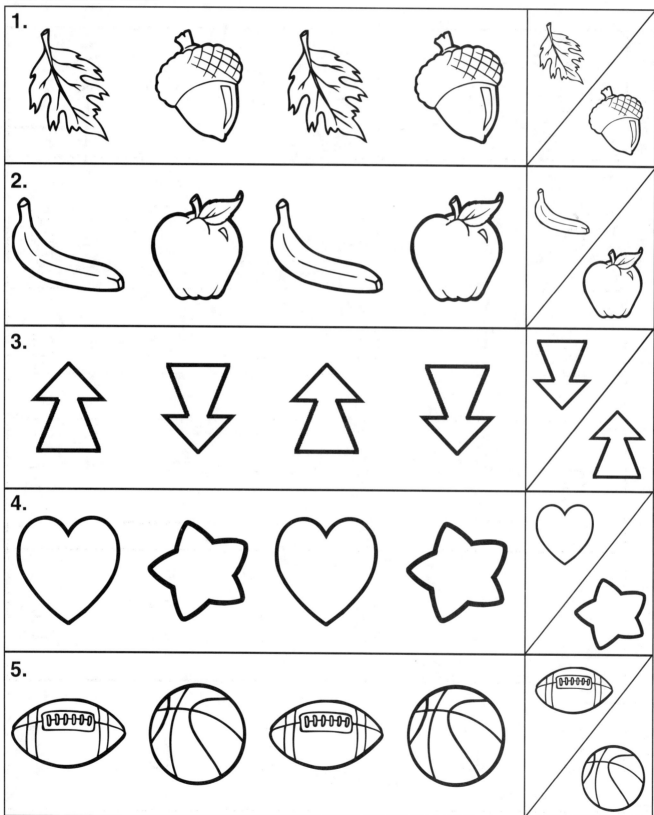

Patterns with Numbers

Directions: Look at each line of number patterns. Write the missing number on each line to complete the pattern.

1. 0 1 0 1 0 ___

2. 6 7 8 ___ 7 8

3. 3 ___ 4 3 4 4

4. 9 8 7 9 ___ 7

5. ___ 2 3 1 2 3

6. 5 6 ___ 5 6 7

What Comes Next?

Directions: Look at the pattern in each row. Complete the pattern by drawing what comes next.

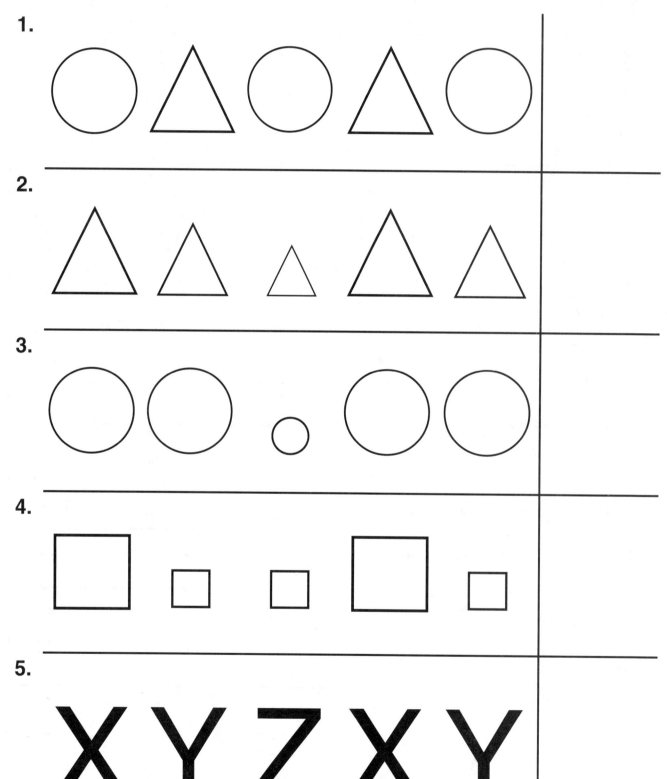

1.

2.

3.

4.

5.

X Y Z X Y

Shapes of Different Sizes

Directions: Draw a line from each shape to the word that names the shape. Each word will have more than one shape.

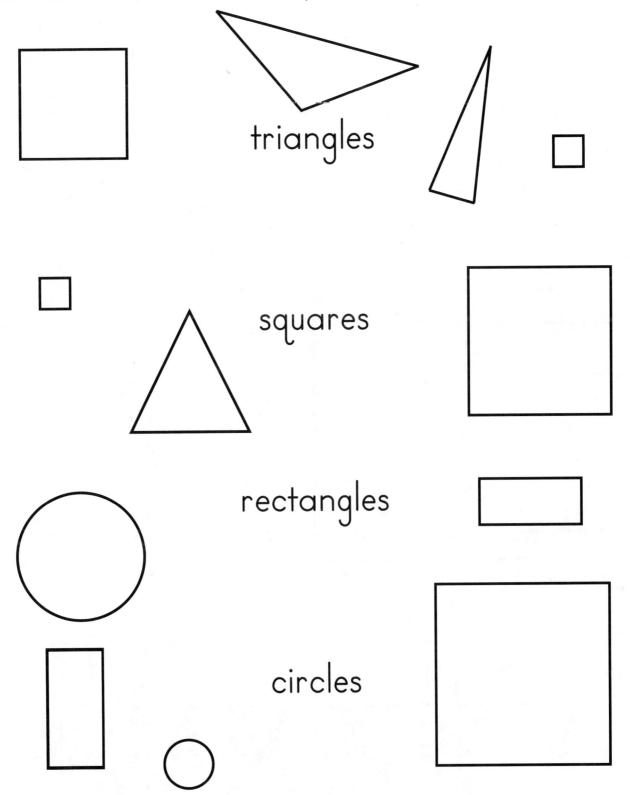

triangles

squares

rectangles

circles

Geometry

Name the Shapes

Directions: Write the name of each shape on the line below it. Use the words from the word bank to help you.

rectangle	diamond	triangle
square	circle	oval

1.

4.

2.

5.

3.

6.

#2740 Mastering Kindergarten Skills   146   ©Teacher Created Resources, Inc.

Corners and Sides

Directions: Count how many corners and sides are on each shape. Record the numbers below.

1.

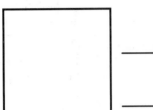

_____ corners

_____ sides

5.

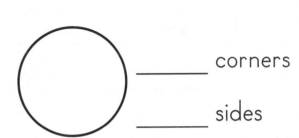

_____ corners

_____ sides

2.

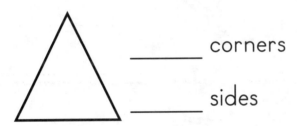

_____ corners

_____ sides

6.

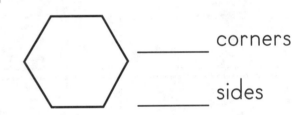

_____ corners

_____ sides

3.

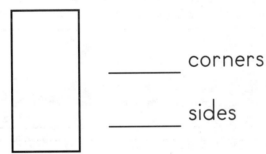

_____ corners

_____ sides

7.

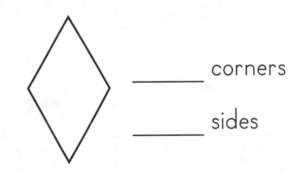

_____ corners

_____ sides

4.

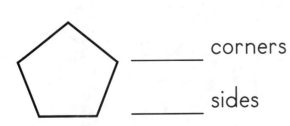

_____ corners

_____ sides

8.

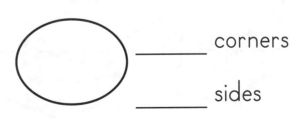

_____ corners

_____ sides

3-D Shapes

Directions: Say the name of the shape in the first box. Color the objects in each row that are the same shape as the shape in the first box.

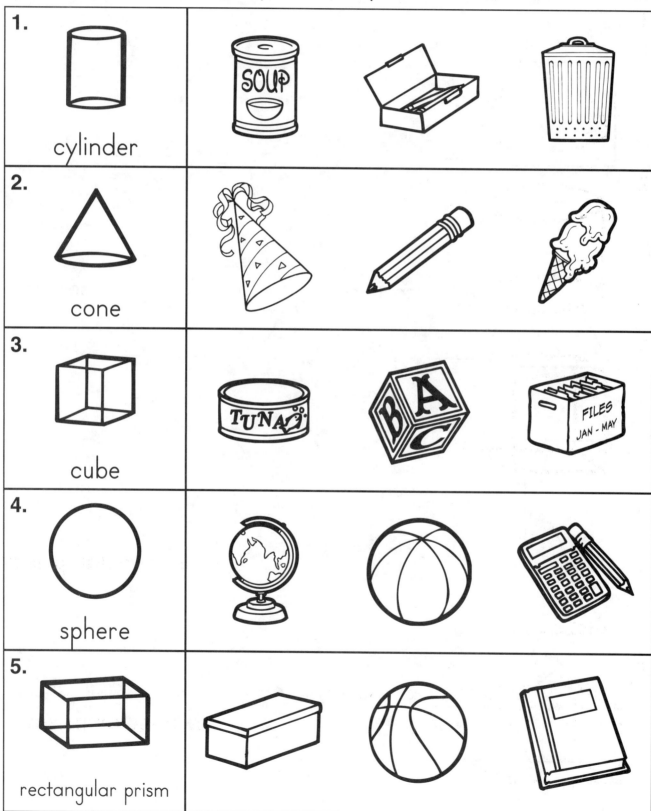

1. cylinder
2. cone
3. cube
4. sphere
5. rectangular prism

3-D Shape Match

Directions: Draw a line to match each shape to its name.

1.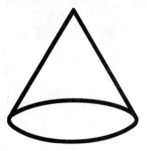

cube

2.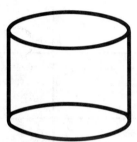

cone

3.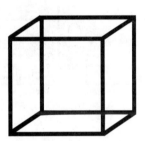

cylinder

4.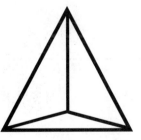

rectangular prism

5.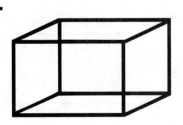

triangular prism

Reading a Calendar

Directions: Use the calendar to answer the questions.

October						
Sun.	Mon.	Tues.	Wed.	Thurs.	Fri.	Sat.
				1	2	3
4	5	6	7	8	9	10
11	12 Thanksgiving Day	13	14	15	16	17
18	19	20	21	22	23	24
25	26	27	28	29	30	31 Halloween

1. What is the name of the month? _____

2. How many days are in the month? _____

3. What day of the week is the 18th? _____

4. How many Tuesdays are in this month? _____

5. What day is Thanksgiving? _____

Days of the Week

Directions: Write the names of the days of the week in the correct order. Use the words in the Word Bank to help you.

Sunday
Tuesday
Saturday

Word Bank
Sunday
Tuesday
Saturday
Monday
Friday
Wednesday
Thursday

Color the boxes that name weekdays **blue**.

Color the boxes that name the weekend **red**.

Time

Months of the Year

Directions: Write the names of the months of the year in the correct order. Use the **Word Bank** to help you.

Word Bank			
April	December	June	February
September	January	October	May
March	July	August	November

1. _____

2. _____

3. _____

4. _____

5. _____

6. _____

7. _____

8. _____

9. _____

10. _____

11. _____

12. _____

Telling Time

Directions: Read the time on each clock. Circle the correct time below.

1.

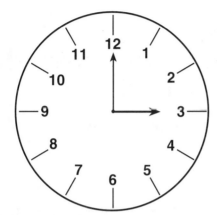

3:00   6:00

4.

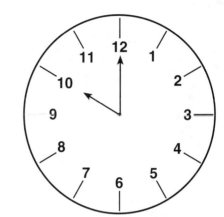

10:00   1:00

2.

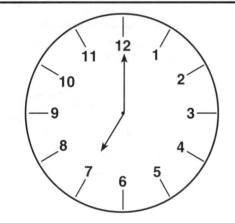

12:00   7:00

5.

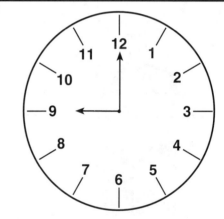

3:00   9:00

3.

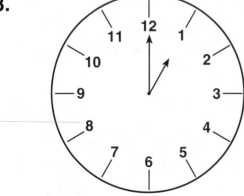

2:00   1:00

6.

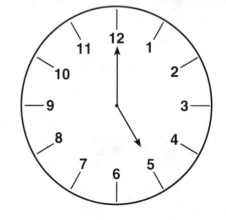

8:00   5:00

Match the Clocks

Directions: Draw a line to match the clocks that show the same time.

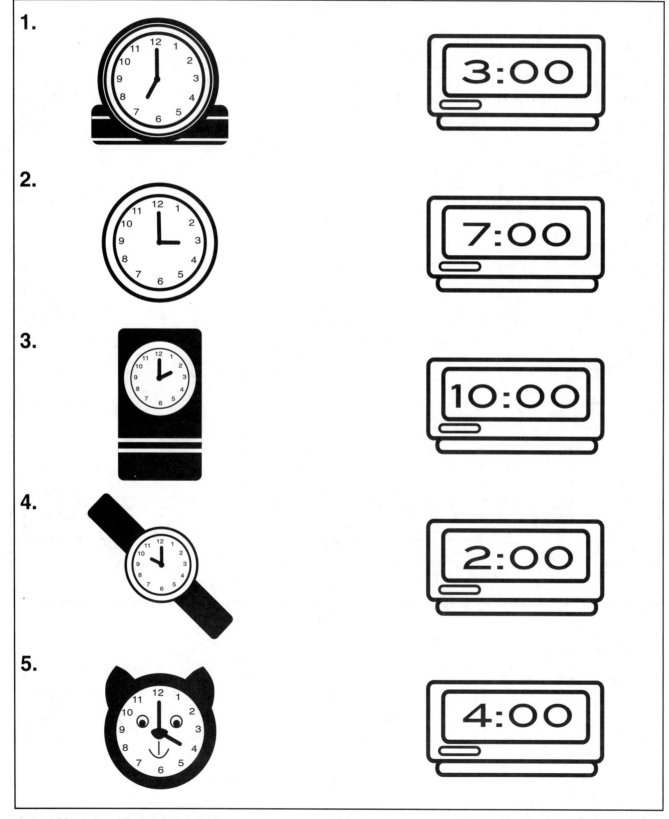

154

What Time Is It?

Directions: Write the time shown on each clock.

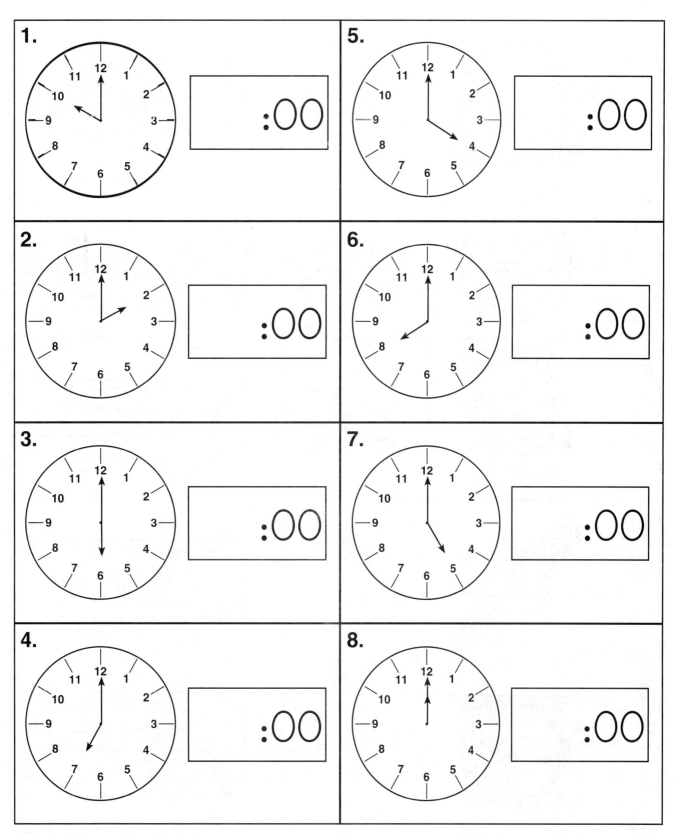

Longest and Shortest

Directions: Color the longest object in each row. Circle the shortest object in each row.

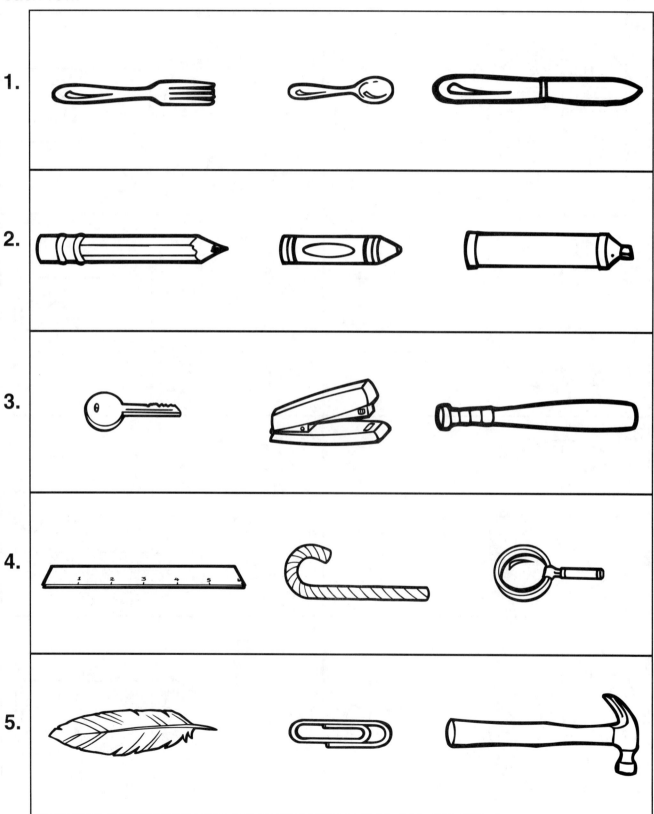

1.

2.

3.

4.

5.

Biggest and Smallest

Directions: Color the biggest object in each row. Circle the smallest object in each row.

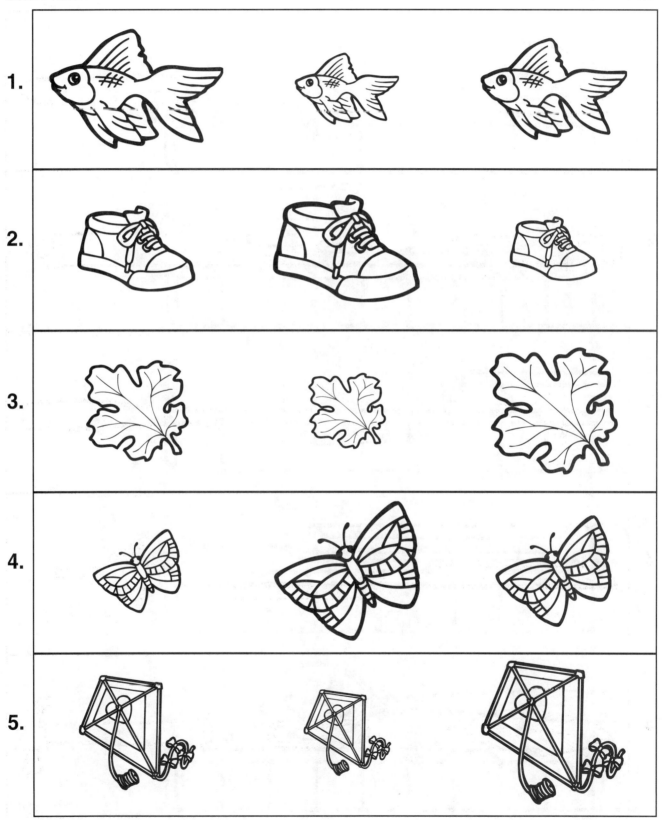

How Long?

Directions: Measure how many cubes long each object is. Write the number.

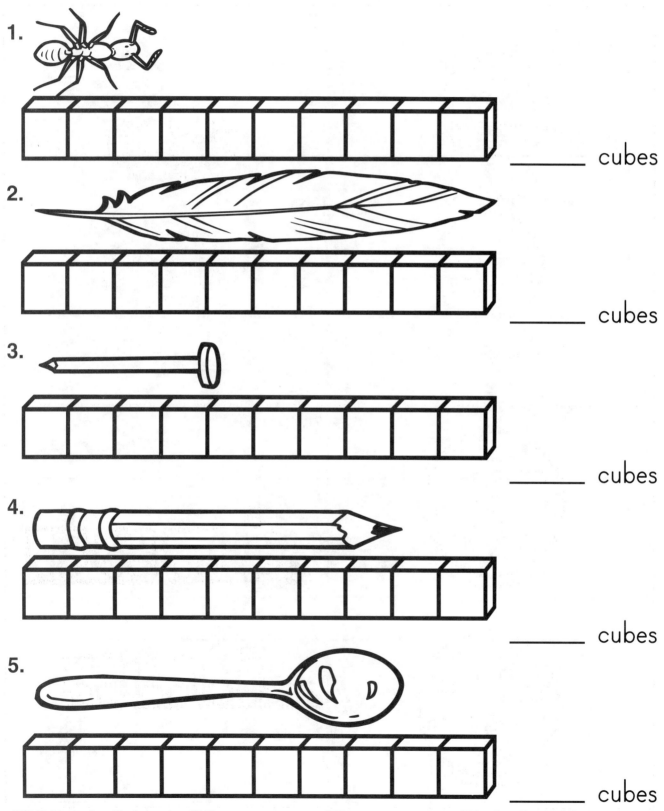

1. _____ cubes

2. _____ cubes

3. _____ cubes

4. _____ cubes

5. _____ cubes

Least and Most

Directions: Compare each pair of pictures. Color the picture that has the most. Circle the picture that has the least.

1.

2.

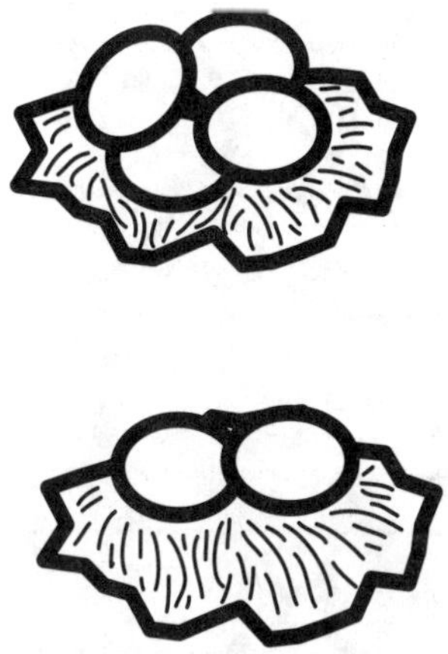

3.

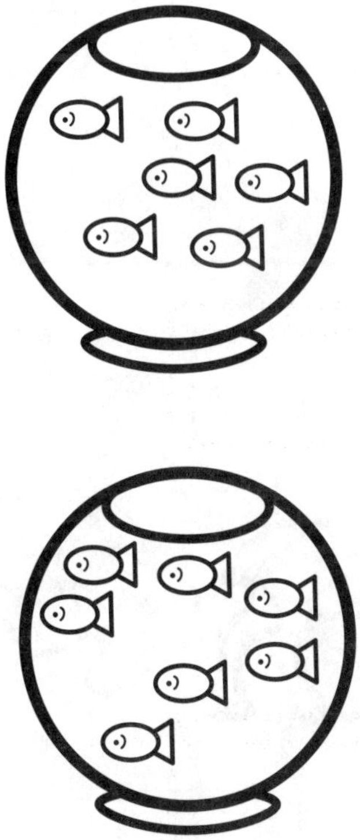

4.

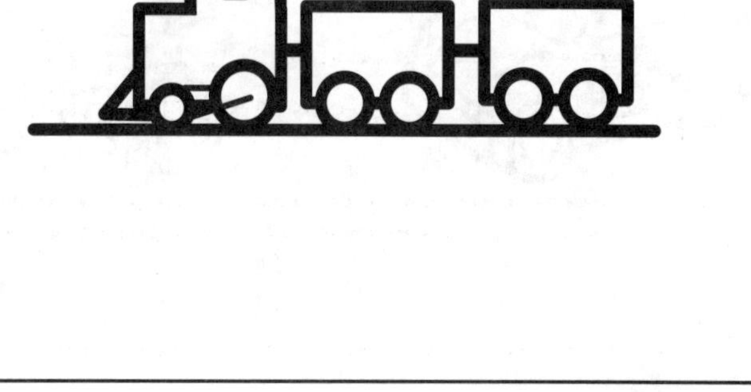

Fast and Slow

Directions: Look at each pair of pictures. Circle the picture that shows **fast**. Color the picture that shows **slow**.

1.

4.

2.

5.

3.

6.

160

In and Out

Directions: Color the toys that are **in** the box.

Directions: Color the toys that are **out** of the box.

The Candy Jar

Directions: Count the items in the picture. Complete the graph by coloring one box for each item counted.

Graphing

Going to the Park

Directions: Count the items in the picture. Write the numbers on the lines. Complete the graph by coloring one box for each item counted.

©Teacher Created Resources, Inc.　　　163　　　#2740 Mastering Kindergarten Skills

It's Different

Directions: Look at the pictures in each row. Color the three pictures that are the same. Draw an **X** on the picture that is different.

164

Ball Match

Directions: Look at the patterns on the marbles. Match the marbles on the left to the marbles on the right.

1.

2.

3.

4.

5.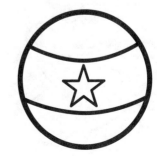

Tea Time

Directions: Look at the teapots and cups. Draw a line from the teapot on the left to its matching cup on the right. Color the teapots and the matching cups.

1.

2.

3.

4.

5.

Complete the Picture

Directions: Look at the picture on the top. Draw the missing items to complete the picture on the bottom so that both pictures match.

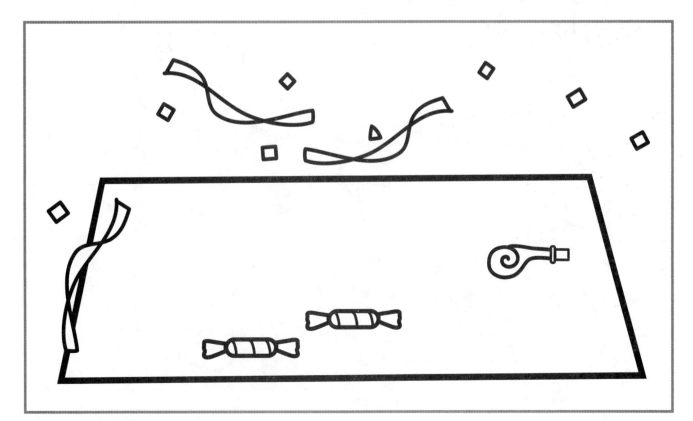

What's Missing?

Directions: Complete each picture by drawing the missing parts.

1.

2.

3.

4.

5.

6.

Opposites

Directions: Draw lines to match the opposites.

1.    

2.    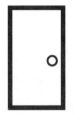

3.    

4.    

5.    

6.    

Painting a Picture

Directions: Show the correct order of the story by writing the numbers 1, 2, 3, and 4 in the correct boxes.

170

Baking Bread

Directions: Show the correct order of the story by writing the numbers 1, 2, 3, and 4 in the correct boxes.

Answer Key

Page 4

Students should have colored the child sitting at a desk and reading, the child sitting in the chair with the book in her hands, the child placing a book on the bookshelf, the child returning a book to the library, and the child listening to a story on her parent's lap.

Page 5

1. *The Little Hungry Ant*
2. 4
3. Nan James

Page 6

Letters (circled)—A, C, v, L, q, f, t, r, W, z
Numbers (an X)—3, 5, 7, 4, 2, 8
Words (underlined)—dog, yes, no, cat

Page 7

1. 2	3. 4	5. 3	7. 3	9. 3
2. 3	4. 3	6. 4	8. 4	10. 4

Page 8

1. b	3. n	5. a	7. i	9. b	11. b
2. l	4. d	6. o	8. u	10. p	12. n

Page 9

1. word   3. sentence   5. letter   7. word
2. letter 4. word   6. sentence 8. letter

Page 10

1. 4   2. 5   3. 4   4. 5   5. 4

Page 12

1. 1	3. 1	5. 2	7. 1	9. 2	11. 2
2. 2	4. 4	6. 1	8. 3	10. 1	12. 2

Page 13

1. same sound   6. same sound
2. same sound   7. different sounds
3. different sounds   8. same sound
4. same sound   9. same sound
5. different sounds

Page 14

Answers indicate the one that has a different sound.

1. lemon   3. pencil   5. present
2. mitten   4. fox   6. turtle

Page 15

Answers indicate the words that end with the same sound.

1. ax, fox, box   4. jet, cat, knot
2. bag, leg, hug   5. top, cup, lip
3. can, sun, pin   6. gum, vacuum, jam

Page 16

1. ends with n   5. begins with n
2. begins with n   6. ends with n
3. begins with n   7. ends with n
4. ends with n   8. begins with n

Page 17

1. same sound   7. same sound
2. different sound   8. same sound
3. same sound   9. different sound
4. same sound   10. same sound
5. different sound   11. different sound
6. same sound   12. same sound

Page 18

1. rhyme   5. rhyme
2. rhyme   6. do not rhyme
3. do not rhyme 7. rhyme
4. rhyme   8. rhyme

Page 19

1. hat, bat, rat   4. pen, hen, men
2. hug, rug, jug   5. cap, clap, wrap
3. pop, top, hop

Page 22

Ff, Kk, Mm, Bb, Ee, Gg, Tt, Hh, Nn, Rr

Page 23

1. b	9. D
2. f	10. Y
3. n	11. Q
4. r	12. H
5. e	13. L
6. m	14. W
7. c	15. G
8. k	16. T

Page 26

Students should color the ax, astronaut, apron, and alligator.

Page 29

Students should color the duck, dog, donut, and dinosaur.

Page 30

Students should color the elephant, ear, elbow, and envelope.

Page 31

Students should color the feather, fire, five, and fork.

Page 33

Students should color the house, hose, hammer, and hat.

Answer Key (cont.)

Page 34
Students should color the ink, iron, and the iguana.

Page 35
Students should color the jet, jar, jeep, and "juggle."

Page 38
Students should color the mitten, mask, mop, and monkey.

Page 40
Students should color the ostrich, oboe, octopus, and octagon.

Page 41
Students should color the pen, pin, pumpkin, puppy, and pillow.

Page 45
Students should color the tie, tiger, tooth, and tent.

Page 46
Students should color the umpire, "up," uniform, and "under."

Page 47
Students should color the vase, violin, vest, and volcano.

Page 49
Students should color the ax, fox, box, and six.

Page 52
1. ball and bee
2. fox and fish
3. leaf and lion
4. monkey and man
5. rabbit and rainbow
6. sun and six

Page 53
1. f   5. z   9. d   13. v
2. m   6. t   10. l   14. k
3. b   7. w   11. s   15. f
4. r   8. h   12. p   16. j

Page 54
1. z   3. l   5. t   7. t   9. p   11. s
2. m   4. k   6. h   8. b   10. w   12. r

Page 55
1. top, ten, tub, tap, tug
2. bed, bat, bell, ball, bun
3. map, mug, men, mop, mad
4. ring, rug, rat, rock, rip
5. pig, pot, pen, pan, pop

Page 56
1. hop, mop, top
2. hug, rug, jug
3. hen, men, pen
4. cap, map, tap

Page 57
1. van
2. tub
3. sun
4. hat
5. net
6. lip

Page 58
1. jet   3. hat   5. pin   7. dot
2. dog   4. sun   6. ten   8. map

Page 59
1. m   5. l   9. d   13. n
2. r   6. t   10. s   14. d
3. x   7. n   11. x   15. p
4. k   8. f   12. g   16. b

Page 60
1. fan   3. cub   5. log   7. sun   9. dot
2. map   4. pen   6. pin   8. web

Page 61
1. map, man   3. hut, hug   5. ham, hat
2. dot, dog   4. web, wet   6. cap, cat

Page 62
1. bed   3. hut   5. pen   7. cot
2. dog   4. fin   6. map   8. rug

Page 63
1. wig   4. net   7. lid   10. pen
2. mop   5. bed   8. pot   11. rug
3. jam   6. tub   9. map   12. lip

Page 64
1. middle   9. middle
2. end   10. end
3. middle   11. end
4. end   12. beginning
5. middle   13. end
6. beginning   14. beginning
7. beginning   15. middle
8. middle   16. beginning

Page 65
1. map   3. van   5. sad   7. bag
2. hat   4. ham   6. cab   8. bat

Page 66
1. A dad has a van.   3. A rat has a can.
2. A cat has a map.   4. A man has a hat.

Page 67
1. hen   3. nest   5. bell   7. bed
2. jet   4. men   6. ten   8. net

Page 68
1. The hen has a bell.   3. The men have a net.
2. Ned is wet.   4. The nest has eggs.

Page 69
1. pin   3. ring   5. pig
2. wig   4. hill   6. lid

Page 70
1. The king can sit.   3. The kid has a bib.
2. The kid can dig.   4. The pin will fix the rip.

Page 71
1. dot   4. hop   7. cot   10. hog
2. pop   5. dog   8. top   11. rock
3. log   6. sock   9. lock   12. pot

Answer Key (cont.)

Page 72
1. The dog is on a log.
2. The dog can jog.
3. The dog is on top.
4. The dog can mop.

Page 73
1. nut   3. sub   5. hug   7. tub
2. bug   4. sun   6. hut   8. mug

Page 74
1. The cub can run.
2. The bug is in the sun.
3. The tub is on the rug.
4. The mug is by the bun.

Page 75
1. e   3. i   5. o   7. e   9. u   11. i
2. u   4. a   6. a   8. o   10. i   12. e

Page 76
1. a   3. a   5. o   7. e   9. o
2. e   4. u   6. i   8. e

Page 77
Short A – dad, sat, tan   Short E – fed, yet, den
Short O – fog, hop, lot   Short I – tin, did, pit
Short U – hum, run, dug

Page 78
1. mail, tail   3. gate, skate
2. cake, rake   4. rain, train

Page 79
1. leaf   3. bee   5. key   7. seal
2. feet   4. eel   6. tea   8. meat

Page 80
1. long   3. short   5. short   7. long   9. long
2. long   4. long   6. long   8. short

Page 81
Students should color the boxes with the following
pictures: boat, cone, hose, bow, blow, row, rope, and goat.

Page 82
1. short   4. short   7. long   10. long
2. short   5. long   8. short
3. long   6. short   9. long

Page 83
1. i   3. a   5. e   7. u   9. i   11. o
2. e   4. o   6. o   8. a   10. e   12. u

Page 84
1. bat, cat   3. log, dog   5. bun, sun
2. net, jet   4. wig, pig   6. bell, yell

Page 85
Students should color the following socks the
same color: hat and bat, met and vet, fin and win,
hit and sit, lot and got, run and fun, lap and rap,
red and fed, jog and fog, fig and big, nut and cut.

Page 86
1. win, tin, fin, bin   3. wet, get, let, met
2. mop, hop, pop, cop   4. tug, bug, hug, jug

Page 87
1. top, pop, hop, answers will vary but must end in "op."
2. tap, cap, lap, answers will vary but must end in "ap."
3. cat, hat, mat, answers will vary but must end in "at."
4. men, pen, hen, answers will vary but must end in "en."

Pages 88–91
Students' answers will vary.

Page 96
1. yellow   3. red   5. green   7. black
2. orange   4. brown   6. purple   8. blue

Page 97
1. circle   3. triangle   5. rectangle
2. square   4. heart   6. oval

Page 98
1. eight   3. five   5. six   7. four
2. three   4. one   6. two   8. seven

Page 100
1. 2 hearts   5. 4 flowers
2. 1 balloon   6. 6 crayons
3. 7 smiley faces   7. 3 stars
4. 5 balls   8. 10 dots

Page 116
1. 8   3. 7   5. 10   7. 5
2. 9   4. 12   6. 6   8. 11

Page 117
1. Students should draw 1 starfish.
2. Students should draw 2 shovels.
3. Students should draw 3 suns.
4. Students should draw 4 shells.
5. Students should draw 5 fish.

Page 118
1. Students should color 1 seashell.
2. Students should color 2 crabs.
3. Students should color 3 seastars.
4. Students should color 4 fish.
5. Students should color 5 seahorses.

Page 119
1. 11   3. 14   5. 20 pairs   7. 15   9. 12
2. 19   4. 17   6. 13   8. 18   10. 16

Page 120
1. 11 (more), 6 (less)   3. 7 (less), 10 (more)
2. 7 (more), 6 (less)   4. 6 (less), 9 (more)

Answer Key (cont.)

Page 121
1. Students should draw a set of 6.
2. Students should draw a set of 8.
3. Students should draw a set of 3.
4. Students should draw a set of 7.
5. Students should draw a set of 9.

Page 122
1. Students should draw 6 more teeth.
2. Students should draw 4 more hats.
3. Students should draw 1 more star.
4. Students should draw 2 more olives.
5. Students should not draw anything else.
6. Students should draw 3 more balloons.

Page 123
The following numbers should be circled:
1. 10	3. 8	5. 20	7. 13	9. 11	11. 19
2. 4	4. 12	6. 17	8. 5	10. 16	12. 20

Page 124
1. 1, 2, 3, 4, 5, 6, 7, 8, 9, 10   3. 2, 4, 6, 8, 10
2. 2, 4, 6, 8, 10   4. 2, 4, 6, 8, 10

Page 125
2, 3, 4, 5, 6, 7, 8, 9, 10
5, 10

Page 126
1. 5	2. 2	3. 7	4. 3	5. 6

Page 127
1. 3	3. 4	5. 5	7. 6
2. 5	4. 3	6. 4	8. 5

Page 128
1. 5	3. 5	5. 6	7. 4
2. 3	4. 5	6. 6	8. 4

Page 129
1. $3 + 2 = 5$ 3. $2 + 2 = 4$ 5. $3 + 3 = 6$
2. $2 + 3 = 5$ 4. $1 + 2 = 3$ 6. $1 + 3 = 4$

Page 130
1. 5	3. 3	5. 1	7. 4
2. 2	4. 4	6. 3	8. 2

Page 131

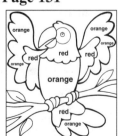

Page 1t32
1. 6	3. 8	5. 9	7. 10	9. 8
2. 8	4. 10	6. 9	8. 9	10. 9

Page 133
1. 1	2. 3	3. 5	4. 2	5. 0

Page 134
1. 2	3. 1	5. 1
2. 3	4. 1	6. 2

Page 135
1. 3	3. 2	5. 1
2. 2	4. 1	6. 3

Page 136
1. $5 - 2 = 3$ 4. $4 - 2 = 2$
2. $3 - 1 = 2$ 5. $5 - 3 = 2$
3. $2 - 1 = 1$ 6. $3 - 2 = 1$

Page 137
1. 4	3. 3	5. 6
2. 5	4. 1	6. 2

Page 138

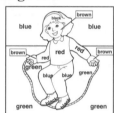

Page 139
1. 3	3. 1	5. 6
2. 5	4. 4	6. 2

Page 140
1. 7	3. 8	5. 10
2. 9	4. 5	6. 10

Page 141
1. 10¢, yes   3. 3¢, bubbles
2. 10¢, yes   4. 10¢, yes

Page 142
1. leaf   4. heart
2. banana   5. football
3. up arrow

Page 143
1. 1	3. 4	5. 1
2. 6	4. 8	6. 7

Page 144
1. triangle   3. small circle   5. Z
2. small triangle   4. small square

Page 146
1. rectangle   3. triangle   5. diamond
2. circle   4. square   6. oval

Answer Key (cont.)

Page 147
1. 4, 4   5. 0, 0
2. 3, 3   6. 6, 6
3. 4, 4   7. 4, 4
4. 5, 5   8. 0, 0

Page 148
1. can of soup, trashcan   4. globe, ball
2. party hat, ice-cream cone   5. shoe box, book
3. block, box

Page 149
1. cone   4. triangular prism
2. cylinder   5. rectangular prism
3. cube

Page 150
1. October   4. 4
2. 31   5. Monday, October 12
3. Sunday

Page 151
Sunday, Monday, Tuesday, Wednesday,
Thursday, Friday, Saturday
Weekdays: Monday, Tuesday, Wednesday,
Thursday, Friday
Weekend: Saturday, Sunday

Page 152
1. January   7. July
2. February   8. August
3. March   9. September
4. April   10. October
5. May   11. November
6. June   12. December

Page 153
1. 3:00   3. 1:00   5. 9:00
2. 7:00   4. 10:00   6. 5:00

Page 154
1. 7:00   3. 2:00   5. 4:00
2. 3:00   4. 10:00

Page 155
1. 10:00   3. 6:00   5. 4:00   7. 5:00
2. 2:00   4. 7:00   6. 8:00   8. 12:00

Page 156
1. Longest – knife, Shortest – spoon
2. Longest – pencil, Shortest – crayon
3. Longest – baseball bat, Shortest – key
4. Longest – ruler, Shortest – magnifying glass
5. Longest – hammer, Shortest – paper clip

Page 158
1. 3 cubes   3. 4 cubes   5. 8 cubes
2. 10 cubes   4. 8 cubes

Page 160
1. Fast – rabbit, Slow – snail
2. Fast – kangaroo, Slow – turtle
3. Fast – race car, Slow – tricycle
4. Fast – cheetah, Slow – baby
5. Fast – jet, Slow – bike
6. Fast – deer, Slow – hippopotamus

Page 162

Page 163

Page 164
1. put X on fourth clown
2. put X on first pizza
3. put X on second book
4. put X on first doll
5. put X on on third horse

Page 168
1. add wings   4. add ears
2. add face   5. add petals and leaf
3. add door   6. add wing

Page 169
1. closed door   4. cold
2. sad face   5. old
3. arrow pointing down   6. night

Page 170
3, 2
1, 4

Page 171
2, 3,
4, 1